BEAR VIEWING IN

ALASKA

BEAR VIEWING IN
ALASKA

Expert Techniques for a Great Adventure

Stephen F. Stringham, PhD

Photography by Kent Fredriksson

GUILFORD, CONNECTICUT
HELENA, MONTANA

AN IMPRINT OF THE GLOBE PEQUOT PRESS

Copyright © 2007 Stephen F. Stringham

Photographs copyright © 2007 Kent Fredriksson

Text design by Sue Murray
Map by M. A. Dubé

Library of Congress Cataloging-in-Publication Data
Stringham, Stephen, 1946–
  Bear viewing in Alaska : expert techniques for a great adventure / Stephen F. Stringham.
    p. cm.
  Includes bibliographical references and index.
  ISBN-10: 0-7627-3953-3
  ISBN-13: 978-0-7627-3953-0
  1. Bears—Alaska. I. Title.
  QL737.C27S827 2007
  599.7809798—dc22

                                                        2005033758

Manufactured in the United States of America
First Edition/First Printing

DEDICATION

Bob and Joyce Stringham
Jacqueline W. Stringham
Christine Nicoyaleff
Jeanette Otti
Helen Strauss
Laura Lippincott
Alan and Marion Solbert

1. Wolverine Creek
2. Tuxedni Bay
3. Silver Salmon
4. Chinitna Bay
5. Chenik
6. McNeil River State Game Sanctuary
7. Wood River and Wood Tikchik State Park
8. Funnel and Moraine Creeks
9. Brooks River
10. Mount Douglas
11. Hallo Bay
12. Kukak
13. Kaflia
14. Kuliak, Missiak, and Kiniak Bays
15. Geographic Harbor
16. Chignik-Black Lakes and Ivanof Valley
17. Yakutat and Glacier Bay National Park
18. Admiralty Island National Monument
19. Kupreanof and Kuiu Islands
20. Baranof Island and Lake Eva
21. Koskiusko Island
22. Anan Creek
23. Margaret Creek and Traitor's Cove
24. Misty Fiords National Monument

CONTENTS

Warning and Disclaimer viii

Preface ix

Acknowledgments xiii

Part I: Getting Started

Chapter 1: Who's Who in the Bear World 1

Chapter 2: What Kind of Bear Is That? 5

Chapter 3: How Safe Is Close Viewing? 11

Chapter 4: What Kind of Experience Do I Want? 15

Part II: Finding Viewable Bears

Chapter 5: How to Select a Viewing Site 21

Chapter 6: Viewing Locations 29

    Churchill, Manitoba 31

    Wrangel Island 31

    Spitsburgen Island 32

    Interior Alaska 32

    Coastal Alaska 32

    Upper Alaska Peninsula, Bristol Bay,

        and Central Katmai National Park/Preserve 38

    Shelikof Strait and the East Flank of the Alaska Peninsula 39

    Western Flank of the Alaska Peninsula....................................43

    Kodiak Island 44

    Kenai Peninsula and Prince William Sound 44

    Wrangell-St. Elias and Kluane National Parks 46

    Southeast Alaska 46

    Coastal British Columbia 55

    Interior of Southern Canada and the Contiguous U.S............56

Part III: Making the Most of Your Trip

Chapter 7: Choosing a Guide..63

Chapter 8: Travel Tips 69

Chapter 9: Essential Equipment and Supplies 77

Chapter 10: Minimizing Risk and Impact 83

Part IV: Conclusion..99

WARNING AND DISCLAIMER

The techniques and products described herein, meant to minimize the risk of bear-inflicted injury, are based on a synthesis of current research, writings, and informed opinion. However, because of the unique and unpredictable circumstances of each human-bear encounter, it is impossible to guarantee a viewer's complete safety. As a bear watcher, it is your responsibility to be cautious in bear habitat. Nothing in this book should be interpreted to mean that you can reduce the degree of caution necessary in dealing with bears.

Neither the author of this book nor anyone involved in its publication or sale warranties that following our advice will protect you from injury. We accept no responsibility for keeping you safe from bears or other animals. Not all bear-safety experts agree on everything said in this (or any other) book. To round out your education on bear safety, it would be wise to consult other sources. Keep in mind that research on bear behavior and on detection and deterrent systems continues to provide new insights, approaches, and solutions.

PREFACE

Tips for a Great Adventure

Over the past forty years, the popularity of bear viewing has grown from the hobby of an eccentric minority into a mainstay of many local economies on the northern Pacific coast—regions where bears are typically tolerant, abundant, and easily seen. Areas once visited by no more than a dozen people each year now see thousands of people.

In 1972, when I first studied bears south of McNeil, on the east coast of Katmai National Park, I had large areas entirely to myself. Now there's hardly any good viewing site along the coast that doesn't receive several plane- or boatloads of people each day during good weather. Likewise, thirty-five years ago at Brooks Falls in the center of Katmai, I seldom saw other viewers. Now the falls receives up to 200 visitors per day. Equally popular is Wolverine Creek, southwest of Anchorage, where visitation approaches 10,000 viewers each summer. The Vince Shute Wildlife Sanctuary in Minnesota is already receiving almost 25,000 visitors per year.

For many, this is a once-in-a-lifetime adventure. It needs to be done right the first time. Yet viewers often go away disappointed. They either don't see any bears, or the sightings are too brief, or the bears aren't doing anything more interesting than grazing or sleeping. Or maybe the bears are perfect but viewers can't get within 300 yards of the animals, or fog and rain are so heavy that viewers can barely see past the ends of their cameras.

The difference between success and failure is often a matter of luck. But it can also be a matter of information and preparation. For the best success, wise viewers don't select a viewing site or time until they identify their own goals and expectations, then find answers to the following questions:

- **What are the best viewing sites?** Where are they located? What are the advantages and disadvantages of each? What factors make one site better than another?

- **When are bears best viewed at each site?** Some sites have good viewing for only a couple of weeks per year, a fact that travel agents may not know or which certain unethical lodge owners might not willingly reveal, saying instead that nature is inherently unpredictable. At many sites, periods of prime viewing are quite similar from year to year.

- **How long can the bears be watched and from how close?** Some viewing tours provide only glimpses of bears, perhaps from hundreds of yards away, while others consistently provide long hours of leisurely viewing at close range.

- **Which sorts of bear activity am I likely to see at each site?** Depending on the date, the time of day, or perhaps the tidal cycle, are you most likely to see bears mating, fighting, chasing salmon, or nursing cubs?

- **Do I need a guide?** Unless you are an expert on viewing safety, you probably will.

- **How can I select a guide suited to my needs?** If your first step is to select lodging or transportation, you aren't likely to have much choice in guides. In many cases, a lodge employee or a boat or airplane pilot will serve as your guide. Your trip might be much more fun and successful, however, if you start off by picking a guide. He or she can then help you find the best options for a viewing site, including lodging and transportation.

- **What equipment and supplies should I bring?**

- **What are the basic styles of viewing?** For instance, will I be viewing from an observatory platform, or will I be roaming freely among the bears?

- How safe will the viewing be, and how can I minimize the risk?

In the past, people have usually tried to find this information by consulting magazines, Web sites, or travel agents. But few travel agents know anything about the viewing sites other than what they are told by lodge owners, tour companies, and other local service providers. Even if you contact the local providers personally, you should be aware that a typical lodge or tour company serves only its immediate surroundings. Even the best air taxi service is limited in the geographic areas that it can visit cost effectively. Unless you ask specifically, don't expect even an honest company to warn you, for instance, that most bears are seldom visible for more than a few minutes each day, or that sunny days are very rare compared to rainy, windy ones.

To help the beginning bear viewer avoid the most predictable pitfalls, I have done my best in this book to answer most of the general questions. Of course no one can guarantee you an ideal viewing experience, but knowing what questions to ask will increase your odds of success, as well as minimize your risks.

Many viewing guides come to know their bears on a first-name basis. In September 2005, photographer Kent Fredriksson came up on Cooper (right) and Landy beside Alaska's Russian River.

ACKNOWLEDGMENTS

I am deeply indebted to four kindred spirits: Captain John Rogers, whose generosity made possible my field research at Katmai National Park, as well as Val Geist, Alan Solbert, and David Mattson for decades of sharing their penetrating insights, integrity, and moral support during even the bleakest of times.

If you want to watch bears at Katmai or any other part of the Alaska Peninsula, there is a strong chance that you will fly or boat there from the Kenai Peninsula—the self-styled "Bear Viewing Hub of the World." Before beginning that final leg of your trip, you may need to gather information or stock up on hard-to-find products such as electric fences, pepper spray, and a backpacking raft; you may also need to book a guide and transportation. To ease those tasks, this book directs readers to local sources of these and other products and services. Among those sources are the businesses, organizations, or individuals that sponsored my research and writing. Without their financial or in-kind contributions, this book would never have been written. For further information, consult the Web site of the Bear Viewing Association, www.bear-viewing-in-alaska.info.

Electric fence chargers were provided by Alaska Power Fence (Homer, AK, 907–235–7055) and by UDAP (866–BEAR–911, www.udap.com), which also contributed an ultralightweight "bear shock" backpacking fence. RadioShack (Kenai, AK, 907–283–9020) provided intruder alarms.

Bear deterrent pepper sprays were provided by three manufacturers: UDAP, Katydid, and Pepperball Technologies for testing purposes. UDAP spray was also provided by Eagle Enterprises (Anchorage and Homer, AK, 907–235–7937, lisaw@eaglesafety.net)—the only local source of bear-deterring marine handheld flares, and by Soldotna Hardware (907–262– 8729), which also provided a variety of other field equipment and supplies. Unitech of Alaska (Anchorage, AK, 800–649–5859, carndt@unitechofalaska.com) provided metal bear-proof food barrels (five- and ten-gallon sizes).

Alpacka Raft provided a featherlight craft that has proven invaluable for crossing streams, bogs, and lakes. Rafts and canoes were also made available from Alaska Canoe Rentals (Sterling, AK, 907–262–2331, www.alaskacanoetrips.com). CNK Computer Solutions (Kenai, AK, 907–335–4263, James@cnkcs.net) donated a PC.

Animal skulls, jaws, and teeth for our wildlife courses were provided by Butch and Lisa Bon (Bear & Raven Gifts, 907–841–5867), Ken Jones (Skulls & Bones, Soldotna, AK, 907–260–6592), and Ronnie Aldridge (Caribou Unlimited–Outfitting & Taxidermy, Soldotna, AK, 907–262–7585). Professional photo processing and slide scanning were provided by Ralph Gaines (Nikiski Scientific, 907–398–7094—who also lent us a high-quality camera and lenses. Alaskana Books (907–745–8695) provided classic books on Alaska's wildlife—some of which were otherwise unobtainable.

The Alaska Wildlife Conservation Center (Girdwood, AK, 907–783–2025) allowed us to work directly with two captive black bears and to utilize their superb facilities for observing brown bear, coyote, lynx, red fox, moose, caribou, elk, Sitka deer, bison, and wild boar.

Biolife, LLC (800–722–7559) provided a generous supply of QR (Quick Relief) for stopping bleeding—a product that no one should be without in wilderness or anywhere else that significant injury is likely.

An Iridium sat-phone was provided by Surveyor's Exchange (907–345–6501).

Accommodations were provided by Alaskan Serenity Bed & Breakfast (Soldotna, AK, 800–764–6648, www.alaskanserenitybb.com).

The Bear Viewing Association has awarded uniquely Alaskan jewelry and art to special supporters of bear safety and viewing, including Akihiro Aoki, Alaska's revered counsel general from Japan. That was possible because of generous contributions by artists Maverick Jaillet, Butch and Lisa Lehrman-Bon (Bear & Raven Gifts 907–841–5867), Alaska Horn &

Antler (Soldotna, AK, 907–262–9759), and Custom Seafood Processors (Soldotna, AK, 907–262–9691).

Valuable assistance and insights for bear viewing and safety were provided by John Rogers (Katmai Coastal Tours, 800–532–8338, www.katmai bears.com), John Toppenberg (reflectionsak@alaska.net); Greg Arnold (Alaska Sailing Tours, Soldotna, AK, AlaskaSailing@ak.net, 907–299–7245), Dr. Lynn Rogers (North American Bear Center, www.bear.org), and Dr. Roland Maw. Joseph Kashi (907–262–4604) provided essential legal advice.

Financial donations were provided by some of the above sponsors, as well as by Kenai Peninsula Fishermen's Association (907–2762–2492), United Cook Inlet Drift Association (Soldotna, AK, 800–770–7337), Kenai River Professional Guide Association, Big Sky Charter & Fishcamp (907–262–9496), Silver Salmon Lodge (907–262–4839), Hallo Bay Wilderness Lodge (Homer, AK, 907–235–2237, www.hallobay.com), and Owen and LiLi Shafer.

This tree trunk in a Katmai National Park coastal meadow is a popular spy perch for wolves, foxes, and bears. Over a period of years, this female wolf became quite friendly with Fredriksson and Stringham. Hallo Glacier looms in the background.

At age six months, Snowball, a rare "ghost" grizzly, greets the author and photographer as they arrive at Katmai's Hallo Bay in 2002.

GETTING STARTED

While it is relatively rare, adult male bears do occasionally kill cubs. Mother bears are always wary and quick to drive away any male that ventures too close.

CHAPTER 1

WHO'S WHO IN THE BEAR WORLD

I watched from the shore as a 12-inch rainbow trout fed in the eddy below me. From above, the flecks of red and peach on its flanks were invisible. Only its back was exposed. Except for slight movement of its fins and gills, it might have been just another river stone.

I'd forgotten to bring a fishing pole, so I rigged one from a pine branch, adding the hook and yards of monofilament line that I carried for emergencies. I dug a few worms from the soil and was about to lower my hook into the pool when I caught motion in the corner of my eye. Fifty yards downstream, the tops of a stand of brush began to wave. A huge chocolate-colored animal charged into the clear, cold creek. Chasing fish, the bear splashed belly deep into the water.

I silently exulted. Yes! It was my first glimpse of a wild bear.

I was downwind and hidden in the shade of a huge old ponderosa, screened by roots. The bear stopped its charge less than 5 yards away.

I was delighted to find myself so close; then I was terrified. How long until an eddy of swirling air wafted my scent to the huge carnivore?

The bear cruised the pool, its head dipping briefly underwater as it looked for fish. A fleeing trout finned up a shallow riffle. Two lunges and the bear was there, slapping its paws down to pin the trout. Powerful jaws bit into the struggling rainbow, and blood streamed down the bear's chin as it lumbered ashore.

The bear never looked in my direction. Bending its head to strip the flesh from its fish, the dark brown animal quickly finished its meal. Then it shook its wet fur like a dog, spraying water in every direction. Quiet as a drift of smoke, the hairy angler faded back into the brush. Had it been a black bear in a brown color phase? Or had it been a grizzly? I stopped to think. No shoulder hump, the hips had looked high, and the profile of the face had seemed more convex than concave. A huge black bear.

After a few minutes, I emerged cautiously from my hiding place. Stepping out onto the sunny trail, I stretched my cramped muscles.

It felt so good to be alive.

Over the years, I have viewed hundreds (if not thousands) of bears in the wildernesses of Alaska, Canada, and the Lower Forty-eight, and it's an experience that feels new every time, always somehow magical. No two viewing experiences are ever quite the same.

For a bear viewer, Alaska is mecca. It's the only American state with all three species of North American bear, providing habitat for at least 50,000 black bears *(Ursus americanus)*, 30,000 grizzly/brown bears *(Ursus arctos)*, and 4,000 polar bears *(Ursus maritimus)*. Grizzly/brown bears are found throughout the mainland of Alaska and on the three major islands of the Alaska Panhandle (Baranof, Chichigof, and Admiralty).

Black bears were once distributed over nearly all of forested North America, and while their numbers and range have been reduced, an estimated 600,000 to 900,000 remain, distributed from the Atlantic to the Pacific, Florida to Alaska. In Alaska, they can be glimpsed almost everywhere there are trees, often disappearing into the roadside brush as you're driving to or from Anchorage or Fairbanks. Well aware of where they sit in the chain of command, black bears are rarely seen in the company of grizzly/brown bears.

In North America, grizzly/brown bears were once common west of Hudsons Bay and the Mississippi River, from Mexico to Alaska. Today, the 60,000 that remain live mostly in Canada and Alaska. There are at least 400 grizzlies in the ecosystem around Yellowstone National Park, and there are also grizzlies in the Northern Continental Divide Ecosystem, which encompasses Glacier-Waterton Park. There are also a few grizzlies near the borders between Canada and Washington and Montana and Washington. Alberta, Canada, maintains a population of a thousand or so grizzlies. Elsewhere, they are still abundant only in British Columbia, the Northwest Territory, Yukon Territory, and Alaska.

When talking about grizzly/brown bears, there is no clear genetic or geographic divide between the two types of bears. But *arctos* living inland, far from coastal salmon streams (removed by at least 20 miles), are known as grizzlies. The population of *arctos* living on the coasts of British Columbia and Alaska—typically larger and better fed (and usually less aggressive)—are commonly called brown bears, or "brownies."

Polar bears occupy only the Arctic Ocean and its shores. Alaska's polar bears live on the sea ice and adjacent shores of the Beaufort and Chukchi Seas.

CHAPTER 2

WHAT KIND OF BEAR IS THAT?

Where the territories of black bears and grizzly/brown bears overlap, your first task as a viewer is to identify the species of the bear you're watching. It can be a matter not only of curiosity but of safety.

If you're outside grizzly/brown bear habitat (essentially, east of the Rockies or south of Laramie, Wyoming), then deciding whether the animal you're looking at is a grizzly or a black bear is simple. Regardless of its color phase (brown, blond, cinnamon, etc.), if it's a bear, it's almost certainly a black bear. Where their ranges overlap, however, telling a grizzly from a blackie is a minor, if sometimes vital, challenge. The best way to tell is by considering several characteristics; one trait is seldom enough.

On the Russian River of the Kenai Peninsula, a bear nicknamed Cooper scratches at his ear.

Color phase is an important (albeit inconsistent) indicator. Both species of bear can range from whitish to black, with intermediate shades of brown, cinnamon, blond, or grey fur. However a black bear's fur is usually uniformly colored along the length of the hair whereas the tips of a grizzly's pelt are usually lighter than the rest of the fiber, thus accounting for the common grizzly bear nickname, "silvertip." Confusing matters further, the fur of brown bears (coastal grizzlies) generally lacks the light-colored tip. Coastal grizzlies also tend to be darker in color than their inland counterparts.

In early summer, as bears shed their winter coats, further clues come in the patterning of coloration. The new fur of a grizzly is usually darker in color than the old fur. The legs shed first, the neck last. A partially shed grizzly may have a multitoned coat (for instance a blond body and chocolate legs). By contrast, black bears shed more uniformly, and their old and new fur are similar in color. Any multitoned bear is almost certainly a grizzly/brown bear.

In Alaska, nearly all our black bears are actually black. Rare exceptions are white-colored (Kermode) blackies on the British Columbian coast or bluish grey ones on the upper southeastern Alaskan coast. Blue-grey blackies are known as "blue" or "glacier" bears. Spotting a glacier bear, let alone photographing one, is a rare accomplishment.

When it comes to identifying polar bears, of course, the two most important elements are location and color. Polar bears live only in the Arctic and their fur is white, sometimes with a yellow tint. While grizzlies can seem whitish at first glance, even where the ranges of grizzly and polar bears overlap in the Arctic, polar bears are much whiter and more streamlined. Interestingly, rare grizzly-polar bear hybrids—sometimes called grizzolars—tend to be almost as white as a polar bear, but with a blocky body shape reminiscent of a grizzly. Grizzolars have been bred in captivity, but the first sighting in the wild was in the spring of 2006 when a grizzolar was apparently shot in Canada. Hybridization has been rare in nature because the breeding season of polar bears peaks about one month before that of grizzlies, a time when most polar bears are hunting seals out on the sea ice far from the nearest grizzly. However, with recent

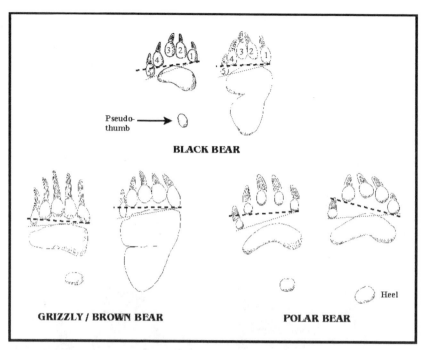

Fig. 1.6. Hand and foot prints of North American bears.
The most obvious difference between the tracks of bear species is the long finger claws of the grizzly. If a fingertip claw is longer than the finger pad, the track was likely left by a grizzly/brown bear. However, if claws are substantially shorter than the fingertip pads, the bear was likely a blackie.

A second method of distinguishing which species made a track is to measure the amount of arch in the arrangement of toe pads. Grizzly/brown bears have the least arch and polar bears the most. This can be seen by running a straight line between the bottom of the first and fourth or first and fifth pads of either hand or foot.

warmer seas and concomitant loss of ice, chances for rutting polar bears to meet and mate with grizzlies may be increasing.

Another good clue in determining a bear's species is the profile of its back. Most grizzlies have a large shoulder hump that is visibly higher than the hips. Polar bears have almost as much hump but higher hips. Black bears have a negligible hump and high hips.

That shape of a bear's face can be another clue. From eyebrows to nostrils, the profile of a grizzly bear's face is slightly concave, or dished, whereas that of a polar bear is slightly convex, or "Roman nosed." The

Polar bears (top row) have a shoulder hump similar to grizzlies but high hips like black bears. This gives them a more streamlined look. Grizzly/brown bears (middle two rows) have prominent shoulder humps and concave faces. The grizzly on the left, second from the top, is an adult female, while the bear next to her is a juvenile. Black bears (bottom row) have higher hips and little or no shoulder hump.

profile of a black bear's face is intermediate between these two.

A more reliable (but less visible) cue for determining species type is the shape and length of the claws on a bear's front paws. A grizzly bear's front paw has claws that can be twice as long as a black bear's. If the claw is longer than the finger pad, the track was likely left by a grizzly bear. Also, the finger pads of a grizzly fall on a line that is much less strongly arced than a similar line drawn for a black bear, and especially for a polar bear. Black and polar bears' finger claws are also more tightly curved and sharper than their grizzly bear counterparts. A grizzly bear's front claws can be up to twice as long as its pad.

CHAPTER 3

HOW SAFE IS CLOSE VIEWING?

Many outdoor enthusiasts look at bears with firmly held prejudices. They believe, for instance, that bears are always unpredictable, that human safety depends on keeping bears and people widely separated, and that the safest bears are those that fear people (thus avoiding them). If all this were universally true, then it would seem that few things would be more dangerous than watching bears from a close distance. We would expect bear viewers to be among the most common victims of bear attack. Not so. On average, no more than three people are seriously injured or killed by bears per year, and bear viewers are far less likely to be among these injured than some other types of outdoorsmen.

This isn't to deny that a few viewers have been killed, usually when they ventured too close to a grizzly, either ignoring its threats or surprising the

All bears should be treated with respect and courtesy, but sow grizzly/brown bears with cubs can be especially unpredictable and aggressive.

bear at close range. However, the vast majority of viewing is done on coastal brown bears or black bears, animals that are considerably more tolerant of human presence than the typical inland grizzly. Tens of thousands of people have watched these bears at relatively close range without incident. With reasonable precautions (beginning with a prudent choice of viewing site and methods), your risk of being mauled while viewing coastal bears is lower than, say, your risk of being injured while traveling to or from a viewing site in an airplane or boat.

The safest place to view bears is obviously from inside your automobile, tour bus, or tour boat. Outside the vehicle, you're going to be at low risk so long as you are in a tightly knit group of *at least* three to five people. For this reason, among others, most guided viewing tours include at least six people, counting the guide.

Some formal viewing sites have an improved bear observatory, usually a platform or tower, that combines the security of a crowd with that of a physical structure. Although the typical observatory is not bear proof, it will usually provide a sufficient psychological barrier to keep most bears away, or at least to decrease their discomfort at having you so close. Risk is only a little higher when you are standing or sitting on an unimproved observatory (e.g., stream bank) at a popular viewing site where bears have learned to expect, respect, and trust people.

As you're hiking to or from a viewing site, especially if you are bushwhacking off a trail—any circumstance in which you could potentially surprise a grizzly—your risk rises dramatically. Especially dangerous in this situation is a mother grizzly with tiny cubs, or a bear defending an animal carcass. These two circumstances cause by far the greatest numbers of serious or fatal bear maulings. By and large, you should keep to those paths and viewing areas where bears expect you to be, thus avoiding undue surprises.

A few other precautions should always be taken as well. For instance, when entering any area frequented by bears, avoid carrying food or anything that smells of food. To minimize risk to children and the physically challenged, keep them with the rest of the group. Don't let kids race around where they might startle a bear or appear to be presenting themselves as potential prey.

As a general rule, coastal brown bears are far more tolerant of people than are inland grizzly bears. Coastal black bears are approximately as tolerant as coastal brown bears, but inland black bears are highly variable. Black bears in the continental United States tend to be fairly tolerant while those in remote parts of Canada and Alaska seem to be more aggressive. As a viewer, you are well advised to focus your attentions on coastal bears.

With just a little bit of care and a lot of common sense, there is no reason why your bear viewing experience shouldn't be as safe as most of your other outdoor pursuits.

Interior grizzlies and coastal brown bears are the same species, Ursus arctos horribilis, but their environments produce animals of different sizes and temperaments. In part because of the abundance of their food sources (including salmon), coastal brown bears tend to be larger and less aggressive than grizzlies.

CHAPTER 4

WHAT KIND OF EXPERIENCE DO I WANT?

In planning your bear viewing trip to Alaska, there are a number of questions you should first ask yourself. What is it about bears that interests me the most? Do I want to watch them feeding? Mating? Sleeping? Do I want to photograph them? Am I after a sense of acceptance by bears or even a feeling of spiritual kinship with them? Do I unwisely look for the thrill of a dangerous encounter? Am I prepared for the unpredictable climate of the north country? Can I protect myself from mosquitoes and no-see-ums one minute and high winds the next? Can I keep my camera equipment safe from rain, even if it pours all day? Do I want to be alone or part of a small group, or would I be content being among fifty other viewers? Would I be satisfied with viewing along a road or on an elevated viewing platform?

Verbalizing what you hope to accomplish and identifying the constraints under which you operate can help assure the success of your viewing adventure.

Its stomach filled after nursing, a drowsy brown bear cub tries to keep its eyes open.

No matter your final goals, when dealing with bears your first priority should be to minimize the risk to yourself and your companions. At the same time, you should also try to limit your potential disturbance to wildlife. Treat any bear you encounter with respect and consideration, allowing it to go about its business undisturbed.

Almost all bear viewers wish to capture the adventure on film or digital memory card. In pursuing the perfect photograph, however, one of the worst mistakes a viewer can make is to try and provoke reactions from a bear—by tossing food or yelling to make it look toward the camera. The desire for dramatic close-ups has led to the mauling deaths of more than one photographer. If you are determined to get "nostril shots," then select a viewing site where bears are comfortable having people within

25 to 50 feet, and where that's permissible. These sites include Wolverine Creek, Chenik Creek, McNeil River State Game Sanctuary, Brooks Falls, Geographic Harbor, Pack Creek, Gunnuk Creek, Cathedral Falls, Margaret Creek, Fish Creek, Marx Creek, Anan Creek, Churchill, Vince Shute Wildlife Sanctuary, or (soon) the North American Bear Center.

If you will be photographing from a boat (for instance, at Wolverine Creek), expect stability to be a problem. If you will be photographing from a vehicle or observatory, expect to be jostled by other people and to have limited room for spreading the legs of a tripod.

Keep in mind as well that being looked at through a camera lens may agitate some bears, especially if they aren't accustomed to cameras. If a bear is disturbed by being stared at, a camera lens might look as if it were a giant eye.

FINDING VIEWABLE BEARS

Ponds like this one, near the Russian River on the Kenai Peninsula, are favorite foraging sites for bears.

CHAPTER 5

HOW TO SELECT A VIEWING SITE

June in Alaska means mating season for brown bears. Hunkered on my heels, I had just spent several hours watching half a dozen bears loll in the warmth of an early summer afternoon. As the sun set, a chilly wind swept down off Hallo Glacier. One hundred yards away, a sow and twin cubs arose, stretching. The cubs bawled until Mom rolled onto her back to let them nurse. Even at that distance, the rumble of their purrs was clearly audible. Fifteen minutes later, these three bears began drifting toward the beach where a rapidly sinking spring tide had exposed a mile-wide sand flat, home to tens of thousands of tasty razor clams.

Pulling on a jacket, I too followed the retreating tide. As the bears foraged, I let my video camera record their actions. Even after the light was gone, I sat and watched, immersed in peace and awe . . . and never-ending wariness.

Two weeks later, the rutting boars had dropped out of sight and the last cubless sow had completed estrus, probably pregnant. Meanwhile the usual summer drought had scorched the succulent and nutty sedge grass, turning it tough and unpalatable to bears. The next set of clamming tides was still half a month away. The huge glacial bowl of Hallo Bay was deserted but for a couple of sow-cub families. Another month would pass before spawning salmon hit this stream. Since this was early July, the nearest place to see bears was Geographic Harbor, quite a few miles south, or possibly on one of the intervening streams where salmon were present. In coastal Alaska, each bay, each valley, hosts its salmon runs at somewhat different times, and each has its own unique scenery and selection of ursine characters.

Keeping in mind your viewing goals and constraints, it's time to plan your own trip, beginning by identifying which type of viewing site might meet your needs.

Viewing from a Vehicle

If you are uncertain about being out in the open with bears, or perhaps have disabilities that make it difficult to hike, you might be most comfortable viewing bears from a vehicle. There are, unfortunately, relatively few destination areas in the north that cater specifically to these needs. For black and grizzly/brown bears, there's Wolverine Creek, Tuxedni Bay, and Denali National Park in Alaska. For polar bears, there's Churchill, Manitoba. In most of these areas, your vehicle will likely not be a private family car, truck, or camper. At Denali and Churchill, the typical vehicle is usually a tour bus. At Wolverine and Tuxedni, your vehicle will be either an open skiff or a pontoon boat. Viewers are generally advised to remain *inside* their vehicle because of the shelter and mobility it provides, and because being in a vehicle means your presence is likely less disturbing to a bear. The downside of viewing from a vehicle is that it limits visibility and photographic opportunities.

Viewing from an Observatory

Second only to viewing from a vehicle, viewing from a formal observatory offers the safest and most comfortable experience.

Most observatory sites are reached only after walking some distance from the point where mechanized transportation ends. Typical hiking distances vary from a few hundred yards to 2 or 3 miles. If you're lucky, you may see a bear or two along the way.

A typical improved observatory is an elevated platform accessed by a ladder or ramp. Some have a roof to protect you from rain and sun. A few are built as blinds to hide the viewers from bears. Alaska has such observatories at Fish Creek, Marx Creek, Margaret Creek, Anan Creek, Pack Creek, possibly Gunnuk Creek, Glacier Meadows at Chinitna Bay, and Brooks River in Katmai National Park. Minnesota has improved observatories at the Vince Shute Wildlife Sanctuary and soon at the North American Bear Center. The NABC will include not only an elevated platform but a room with ground level windows through which people can watch bears.

An "unimproved" observatory is simply a spot where people regularly gather to watch bears. At McNeil Falls, for example, this is a flat spot or "pad" carpeted with gravel on the bank beside McNeil River. Although bears sometimes walk right past the pad within a yard or two of viewers, they don't generally walk across the pad while people are present. They seem to recognize it as human turf and respect its boundaries. There is an analogous site at the mouth of Chenik Creek. In Geographic Harbor, the observatory is a small island against a riverbank. On the southern edge of Glacier Meadow, there's a small area in a line of trees beside the beach.

There are potential downsides to viewing from an observatory, however. Your options may be limited with regard to selecting the angle of your photographs, the lighting, and the background scenery. The lighting might be in your face, or there might be glare bouncing off water. Bad lighting can preclude good photography if your viewing opportunity lasts only a few hours. To avoid problems, when shopping for a guide or tour company, be sure to ask about lighting conditions during the week you expect to be viewing. You might also consult the Web for photos and journals by people who've been there before you. Some photos are labeled with the date and even the time of shooting.

Viewing from the Ground

As a professional bear viewing guide, I've always liked the seashore, especially those estuaries where river mouths are bordered by broad deltas. If the delta is low enough to flood during especially high tides, it will likely be covered with sedge grass, goosetongue, and other favored bear foods. Some of these meadows, such as the ones below McNeil Falls or Hallo Glacier, are grazed by so many bears that a quick glance might mistake them for a herd of cattle. It's in these areas that my clients and I most often watch sows with their cubs, where pairs can be seen courting or mating, and where all the other dramas of ursine life unfold before our eyes. The downside to such sites is that the bears may be too far away for good photographs, at least unless you have enough time to wait until they drift close to you, or unless you are allowed to drift closer to them.

Although some salmon streams tend to concentrate bears at certain sites, most viewing isn't necessarily so limited. Just as bears travel up and down streams looking for fish, viewers may travel the same routes looking for bears. This happens in Cathedral Gorge below the falls, along several creeks on the Katmai Coast, on Karluk, Frazer, and Thumb Creeks on Kodiak Island, and on the Russian and Kenai Rivers on the Kenai Peninsula. It should be said, however, that this is among the most dangerous ways to watch bears. All other things being equal, I would rather avoid any portion of a salmon stream that runs through dense brush or a forest where bears are hard to see from a safe distance. The chance of surprise close encounters is just too high to make it worth the effort and risk.

Timing

If you are like most visitors, your viewing experience will be limited by when you can take a vacation. If this is the case, you'll need to search for a viewing site that offers good opportunities within your time frame.

As a general rule, bears follow their food. When you learn the seasonal availability of certain edible plants, carrion, and salmon, you vastly increase your chance of successfully predicting where bears can be found.

Digging for roots, tubers, and other underground plants occurs primarily just after bears emerge from hibernation in April and May, before the sprouting of new green plants and the growth of new leaves. It is also at this time that bears focus on scavenging for carrion on beaches or avalanche chutes.

During early spring, you can search for bears in areas where carrion concentrates. Although hard to find (not to mention very dangerous), carcasses can sometimes serve as an impromptu viewing site. Road-killed animals may be buried by passing snowplows, remaining there until spring thaw, and ungulates that have died of starvation may be found in "winter yards" such as groves of willow (for moose) or of conifers (for deer). Spring is also a time when winter-killed marine mammals, such as whales or sea lions, most commonly wash ashore, especially on ocean headlands.

Be extremely cautious about stationing yourself near a carcass. Grizzlies in these situations can be particularly aggressive towards intruders. Anyone who stumbles on carrion defended by a bear risks being mauled. You're much better off familiarizing yourself with the cycles of plant growth and trying to predict the movement of bears based on their available forage. The plants most attractive to bears tend to be those richest in easily digestible starch or protein but low in fiber and toxins. Starchy plants in the spring include Indian potato and other species with large tubers, corms, bulbs, or roots—many of which grow on avalanche chutes where bears can be viewed with binoculars or a spotting scope. Protein-rich plants include succulent herbs or sedge grasses found in wetlands.

Rutting activities—including courtship, sparring among males, and breeding—peak during June for grizzly and black bears and during May for polar bears. Sows with tiny cubs are easiest to see after the rut, during July and August.

And then there are the famous salmon runs of Alaska and British Columbia. Between May and November, different species of salmon ascend rivers at different times. The season typically begins with runs of sockeye ("reds") and chinooks ("kings") , followed by chums ("dogs") and humpies ("pinks"), and finally by coho ("silvers"). The timing of the runs depends upon when salmon arrive at the mouth of any given stream as well as when that stream has deep enough water for the fish to swim upstream. The run can also vary according to tidal cycle, in part because of its effect on water depth at the mouth of the streams. At any given viewing site, bears may be abundant during the peak of a salmon run but scarce otherwise.

At McNeil Falls during the peak of the run, up to seventy brownies can potentially be seen all at once. At Brooks Falls, you may see a dozen or so bears. However, before or after the seasonal sites, you may wait for hours to even glimpse one bruin.

High tides can favor salmon runs but low tides allow bears to forage for clams. Extremely low "spring" tides (typically occurring for only a few days a month) are especially productive for bears and viewers alike. Information on tidal levels in most areas of Alaska and British Columbia is available on the Web. In some areas, you can walk to within a hundred yards of clamming bears without disturbing them. I have spent many a pleasant hour watching bears in these areas. A bear clamming may be little more exciting than a bear grazing; but bears on intertidal flats are so clearly visible that this can be a superb opportunity to observe their social behavior.

Any time you view along the coast, make sure a falling tide doesn't strand your boat or airplane; and make sure a rising tide doesn't wash away your boat or trap you against a cliff or on an island.

Clam digging occurs from April through October, but mainly during the few days each month when tides are lowest (check a tide table for dates).

Sugar-rich fruit is usually most abundant during late summer and fall. Oil-rich nuts (outside Alaska) are available mainly during the fall.

Bear viewing opportunities fade away after October 1 when bears have entered into their final phase of gorging prior to hibernation. This is when they are least tolerant of disturbance. Sticking around into early October may have contributed to the deaths of "Grizzly Man" Timothy Treadwell and his fiancée.

Scenery Opportunities

Since most people come to bear viewing with camera in hand, contextual scenery plays a role in judging the quality of a site. A photo of a bear in

Clamming

Anyone who has ever dug for razors knows how quickly they can retreat out of reach. To succeed, you not only have to dig fast but to one side of the clam so that your shovel doesn't break the clam's fragile shell (it's about as tough as a man's thumbnail). Experienced bears avoid breaking shells both while digging out a clam and then while opening it. As best as I can tell, a bear rests the clam on the sand, places a paw atop the clam, then slides its foot sideways, popping the top half of the shell away from the bottom half. Most bears master the trick; but I haven't, despite numerous tries. The shell breaks each time I try to open a clam bear style, and often even when I try to dig up a clam using my fingers. It's humbling to try mastering ursine survival skills.

front of a waterfall, surrounded by bushes covered with bright red elderberries, is generally preferable to one that includes buildings, vehicles, or other people. Before you decide on a particular viewing site, ask your guide or booking agent about those things, or check the Web and brochures for photos showing typical background scenes at each site.

Governmental Regulations

Each national park or other public land administered by a federal or state agency is likely to have regulations and rules limiting how people are allowed behave. To check for recent changes in regulations or rules in any national park, ask for a copy of its annual compendium. Some viewing areas are accessible by anyone. Others, such as McNeil Falls on the Alaska Peninsula or Cache Creek on Admiralty Island, require lottery-drawn permits typically issued several months before the viewing season.

After a quick lemming hunt, this fox amuses himself by watching photographer Kent Fredrikkson.

CHAPTER **6**

VIEWING LOCATIONS

Our airplane bounced gently across the glassy surface of an Alaskan lake. Slowing, it taxied up to a gravel beach. My friend and I stepped off the plane's pontoon, each with our backpack and supply of food. We stood watching as the plane revved and turned into the wind, picking up speed to lift off again.

We hiked to a nearby commercial campground, finding picnic tables and small fire rings, as well as an outhouse, a shelter for firewood, and an axe. Towering over everything else was a miniature log cabin on stilts at least 8 feet high. It was a cache where food could be stored safe from bears. A cool breeze brought with it the smell of rotting fish. A nearby beach was littered with scraps of salmon left by grizzlies, providing a movable feast for dozens of relentlessly scavenging gulls.

In recent years, this particular campground has come to be surrounded by a tall, heavy-duty chain-link fence to keep bears separate from people, but way back then, the only thing separating the campers from the local bruins was prudence and good luck.

My camp was set up before dark, which began around 11:00 P.M. and lasted only a few hours. Gathering enough wood to cook dinner, I laid a light grill across the fire pit and began cooking a pot of lima beans. Not having much odor to them, beans, rice, and instant mashed potatoes have been my dietary staples for years as a backpacker and have never attracted a bear into my camp. On occasions when I've dared eat canned meat, I've heated the unopened can in a pot of boiling water to eliminate odors. Then immediately after eating, I've sealed the can and any other packaging in plastic bags for quick disposal. (Burning cans to incinerate food residues sends food aromas out onto the breeze, inviting furry dinner guests. Incinerating plastic trash is just as hazardous.) Dirty dishes and silverware were also bagged, then later cleaned well away from my tent. To keep my clothes clean, I wore a rain suit while cooking and eating, then sponged it clean immediately after the meal and dishes were done.

In recent years, the National Park Service has recommended separating your camp from your food by at least 100 yards, and both of those spots from your cooking site by another hundred yards, these three sites being like the tips of a triangle. Over thirty years ago, however, we thought nothing of cooking beside or in our tents—a practice which ruined many a camping trip, nearly including mine.

Not long after I ate dinner that evening, I crawled into my tent, snuggled into my sleeping bag, and dozed off.

It seemed as if I had barely closed my eyes before I heard the quiet scrape of feet on soil outside my tent, and then the sounds of sniffing. Terrified, I watched as a curious nose slowly indented the fabric of my tent wall. I squirmed away to the other side of the tent, frantically trying to unzip my sleeping bag. (Older now, and a few years wiser, when camping around bears I seldom zip up a sleeping bag.)

Abruptly, a bear's paw raked itself down the tent wall. One claw cut a foot-long gash. Panicked, not knowing what else to do, I yelled, "Get out of here!" The shadow across the side of my tent startled away, then slowly retreated.

The rest of the night was spent sleeplessly tossing and turning, considering all the ways I might have chosen a better camping site.

Once you have decided how you are most comfortable viewing bears, and at what time of year—after you've verbalized your goals and ambitions—it's time to sit down with a map and decide where you want to go.

Polar Bears

Churchill, Manitoba

The most convenient and inexpensive way to view polar bears is to visit Cape Churchill, on the southwest shore of Hudsons Bay, in Manitoba, Canada. Bears are trapped on the cape each spring as the sea ice melts, escaping only when the sea refreezes in autumn. In October, November, and early December, the town of Churchill ("The Polar Bear Capital of the World") sees a congregation of bears along its nearby beaches. The community has built up a cottage industry around bear viewing, and the amenities of lodging, meals, and transportation are all in place. Once you've arrived in town (via train from Winnipeg, Thompson, or Gillam, or by plane from Winnipeg or Thompson—there are no roads to Churchill), you'll be driven from town to the cape in a "tundra buggie." This is a converted bus mounted on aircraft tires tall enough to elevate its windows out of reach of all but the biggest bears. So long as you keep your arms and head inside, there is little danger. Tundra buggies provide a relatively warm and convenient haven from which you can get a good view of bears and their habitat.

Wrangel Island

While trips to this Siberian island are expensive and difficult to arrange, there are few more exciting places to watch polar bears. Wrangel Island lies in the Chukchi Sea, above Siberia and under the political auspices of Russia (and not to be confused with Alaska's Wrangell Island). It has the highest density of polar bear denning sites in the world, and every few springs, numerous polar bears and hundreds of walrus are trapped ashore by the melting sea ice. The bears subsist by hunting walrus or by scavenging carcasses of walrus crushed during "stampedes" as these animals rush into the ocean to escape bears.

Spitsburgen Island

Polar bears can occasionally be seen on Spitsburgen Island—a possession of Norway, lying in the Arctic Ocean near the North Pole.

Grizzly Bears

Interior Alaska

Most interior grizzlies are widely scattered, unapproachable, and aggressive. For recreational viewers planning a trip, inland grizzlies are not a species on which to hang your hat. You do have a chance of seeing grizzlies (along with a few blackies) on the Dalton Highway that runs from Dead Horse on the Arctic Ocean south to Fairbanks. You can also try Denali National Park—where most visitors never leave the road and most travel is by bus. To reserve a bus seat or campground space *no more than two days before your visit,* contact central reservations: (800) 622–7275 or Denali National Park, Box 9, Denali Park, AK 99755 (907) 683–2294.

Brown Bears

Coastal Alaska

Cook Inlet

Cook Inlet, on Alaska's south central coast, is the state's bear viewing hub. Most viewers first fly into Anchorage, at the northeastern head of Cook, and then travel to the site that best suits their needs and expectations.

Most prime Cook Inlet viewing sites are on the seacoast, where bears gather to dig clams, graze on succulent plants like sedge and goosetongue, or catch spawning salmon ascending coastal rivers and streams.

To enjoy one of the most spectacular vistas imaginable, fly south from Anchorage along Cook Inlet. Your western horizon will be the Chigmit

Mountain Range, a 300-mile string of towering volcanoes (including Spur, Redoubt, and Iliamna) connected by countless lesser peaks and huge bays. You will pass numerous good viewing sites including Wolverine Creek, Silver Salmon, Glacier Meadows, Chenik Creek, McNeil River, Mikfik Creek, and Douglas River. Most of these areas are regularly served by air taxis and boats from the Kenai Peninsula or Anchorage.

Nearly all the Chigmit range is encompassed within Lake Clark National Park. This is said to be the least-visited national park in America, due both to its remoteness and its incredibly rugged terrain. Its eastern and southern borders offer several spots with fine bear viewing.

Wolverine Creek

Mount Spur is the closest volcano to Anchorage, followed by Mount Redoubt. They are separated from one another by a few smaller peaks

Mineral Nutrients

Less than twenty years ago, Redoubt "blew its nose," exploding its jutting eastern face into an ash cloud that extended 40 miles east onto the Kenai Peninsula, covering everything with inches of sandy or powdery ash. Rock powder is also produced by glaciers as they grind mountains into boulders, and boulders into silt so fine it is called glacial flour. Volcanic and glacial powders are scattered by wind and carried by rivers, fertilizing both land and water with mineral nutrients.

At sea, this powder promotes enormous blooms of plankton that turn the water as green as pea soup—a food bonanza for shrimp and other invertebrates that in turn feed salmon or salmon prey. When these salmon ascend rivers to spawn, their bodies carry ashore critical marine nutrients, especially nitrogen. Bears catch the nutrient-rich salmon, leaving scraps for eagles, gulls, ravens, weasels, mink, otter, and a host of other animals too small or weak to catch salmon for themselves. All of these animals deposit dung, thereby enriching the cold, wet soils with nitrogen and assisting the growth of plant life.

and by the eastern leg of Lake Clark Pass. Roughly 5 miles east of the pass is Big River Lake—which is surrounded by four smaller lakes: Wolverine, Fisher, Marten, and Weasel. The five lakes together are called the Big River Lakes.

Wolverine Creek, less 20 feet wide and 1 mile long, drains Wolverine Lake into Big River Lake. It is famous for hosting enormous runs of sockeye salmon. During dry periods, when Wolverine Creek is too low to be navigated by salmon, the fish gather by the thousands in Big River Lake's Wolverine Cove. Here they can be harvested by hoards of anglers and a dozen or so bears. At times, the salmon are so abundant that you can imagine walking across their backs to shore.

All viewing (and fishing) at Wolverine Creek is done from boats, which can get within 10 to 50 feet of the bears. Extreme close-up photos are possible with negligible risk or disturbance to the bears. In fact, most bruins "pretend" to ignore the viewers, some of them limiting their search for salmon by looking to the right or left of nearby people, avoiding eye contact.

Most of the adult females at Wolverine Creek are regulars who have lived and fished there for years. During the summer of 2004 when I guided viewers at Wolverine, the cove was dominated by the middle-aged sow Mona and her six- or seven-year-old daughter, Bayley. That year, Mona had twin yearlings and Bayley had just been impregnated. Also frequenting the site were two of Bayley's recently weaned three-year-olds, Mischa and James, as well as Emmet, a four-year-old male that Bayley had adopted after being "courted" by him for a year—one of the few documented adoptions among bears. A few other adult or adolescent brown bears passed through occasionally. Because these bears are known individually, some guides can relate their histories back several years—turning otherwise anonymous bruins into ursine celebrities. Some people return year after year to see how their furry friends are faring.

Wolverine Cove is also one of the few sites where you can watch black bears interacting with brown/grizzly bears. This doesn't happen often, and most interactions last no more than a few minutes, but if

A mated pair of bald eagles stands watch above their nest.

you're fortunate enough to see it you should treasure the opportunity.

On a particularly lucky day, you might also see a bear hunting beaver, or a beaver working on its lodge. More commonly, you can watch gulls, magpies, and eagles feasting on salmon scraps, eagles feeding the young in their nest, or swans gliding majestically across the milky waters.

Another tributary of Big River Lake is Fisher Creek, flowing out of Fisher Lake. Salmon reach Fisher Lake by ascending first to Wolverine Lake, then swimming up yet another stream. However, some salmon attempt a shortcut by climbing Fisher Falls. Not only are these falls too steep to be climbed by salmon, but those few that try are highly vulnerable to bears. You won't see many bears at Fisher for very long. Yet even when Fisher Cove has no bears, it is a beautiful site and well worth a stopover when you're boating between your plane and Wolverine Cove.

It is not uncommon for Wolverine Cove to be visited by up to thirty boats at once, most of them filled with fishermen. Care and luck are needed to avoid getting people or fishing gear in your pictures. This opportunity to both fish and view bears at close range attracts over 9,000 visitors a year to Wolverine Cove.

Because this site is so close to Anchorage and the Kenai Peninsula (roughly a one-hour flight from each), it can be reached quickly and relatively inexpensively.

Tuxedni Bay

Separating Mount Redoubt from Mount Iliamna is Tuxedni Bay, an area with several fair viewing sites including Horseshoe Cove and Crescent River (an effluent of Crescent Lake and the site of a guest lodge). Unfortunately, these bears tend to be harassed by the presence of fishermen and so are shy. Not only do they avoid people, including viewers, but they may be overly defensive against anyone who moves inland from the beach in an attempt to stalk close for viewing.

Silver Salmon

East of Mount Iliamna is an expanse of meadows, wetlands, and waters, including Silver Salmon Lake. Draining that lake is Silver Salmon Creek, which hosts moderate salmon runs during June and July, as well as a strong silver salmon run during August and September. It's not unusual to see up to two dozen bears in the meadows around Silver Salmon or on the creek. This is one of the best sites to view rutting behavior and mother-cub interactions. One of the main rutting "arenas" is a meadow within sight of two commercial guest lodges.

Chinitna Bay

Mount Iliamna's southern shore is also the southern margin of Lake Clark National Park, just inshore from the edge of Cook Inlet's Chinitna Bay. The major bear viewing area here is Glacier Meadow. You can watch from a small viewing site on the southern edge of the park, or if you book into the nearby lodge, you can view from their observatory, an elevated platform that provides better visibility and more isolation from bears. Brown and occasionally black bears can be seen grazing in the meadow or chasing salmon in a stream cutting through the near side of the meadow. Bears occasionally visit the lodge grounds or forage along the beach.

The western slope of Chinitna Bay is drained by Clearwater Creek. Its upper reaches sometimes offer good viewing.

Chenik

The next good viewing site south from Chinitna is Chenik Creek. It offers superb viewing for a few weeks during midsummer. Brown bears can often be watched and photographed from distances under 50 feet. The site is accessed by boat or aircraft. Extensive rock reefs just offshore make landing planes there risky, so most visitors fly another mile to Chenik Lake, then hike back to the coast.

McNeil River State Game Sanctuary

At the southern end of Cook Inlet is Kamishak Bay. Its main feature is the active volcano Mount St. Augustine. On the western shore of Kamishak is McNeil River State Game Sanctuary, arguably the world's most famous bear viewing site. McNeil bears are under little hunting pressure and large boars abound. Up to seventy brown bears can be seen here at a time— fishing for salmon or competing for fishing sites. Bears do most of their fishing on McNeil River at the famed McNeil Falls—a steep, boulder-strewn stretch of water.

In the old days, when large boars had less protection from hunters, sows with cubs were more common at McNeil Falls. Now, however, only the most dominant or dim-witted sows dare put their youngsters at risk by fishing there. Mothers and cubs are more likely to be seen away from the river, perhaps digging for clams or grazing in beach meadows.

Visiting McNeil requires a permit from the Alaska Department of Fish and Game. Permits are granted by lottery. The application can be down-loaded at www.wildlife.alaska.gov/mcneil/index.cfm. March 1 is the application deadline, although you can apply for a standby slot as late as April. The site is reached by a one-hour flight from Homer on the Kenai Peninsula.

The typical stay is for four days, with a camp usually set up in a meadow near the beach (viewers bring their own tents, equipment, and food). All cooking, eating, and food storage is done in a government cabin.

From the camping area it's a 2-mile hike to the falls. Parties of up to ten people are guided by an employee of the Alaska Department of Fish and Game. Visitors sit on a gravel pad about 20 feet from the river. Bears sometimes pass by within a few feet of the pad, even when it is occupied by people. Indeed, some bears—especially sows with small cubs—rest nearby to avoid harassment by other bears.

As in most areas along the coast, bears are common only during the salmon runs. During the second half of June, a small number of bears gather to catch sockeye salmon on Mikfik Creek. During July, there is a huge run of chum salmon up McNeil River. Scattered bears can be seen through August.

Upper Alaska Peninsula, Bristol Bay, and Central Katmai National Park/Preserve

Much of the Alaska Peninsula (outside of federal lands) is owned by the Bristol Bay Native Corporation. Before venturing onto those lands, obtain written permission. The BBNC has offices in Anchorage (907) 278–3602.

Upper Alaska Peninsula

The stem of the Alaska Peninsula runs almost 150 miles from Kamishak Bay southwest to Bristol Bay. Much of that distance is filled with Lake Iliamna—actually an inland sea—whose tributaries host some of the world's largest runs of sockeye salmon. Although these tributaries are also home to numerous brown bears, the bears are not readily viewable and are wary of people due to hunting pressure.

Wood River and Wood Tikchik State Park

Iliamna drains through the Kvichak River into Bristol Bay. Farther west along that bay is the village of Dillingham, on the banks of the Wood River. Brown bears can be seen at the village dump or by following the Wood

River upstream through a series of lakes. Bears are often spotted along the riverbanks, but there is no information available on any prime viewing sites.

Funnel and Moraine Creeks

Katmai begins several miles south of Lake Iliamna. The northwest portion is a preserve where limited hunting is allowed. The rest of Katmai is a national park where hunting is forbidden.

Some of the bears that fish at McNeil during July spend other parts of the year in the preserve. For example, once finished fishing at McNeil, a bear will sometimes follow the river upstream west and across the mountains, then move northwest a few miles to Funnel and Moraine Creeks. These creeks host not only salmon but world-class trout—fish so fat that they have been described as finned footballs. This is also a great place to watch bears during early summer.

Brooks River

Aside from McNeil and Wolverine Creek, the most famous bear viewing site in Alaska is the Brooks River on the western side of Katmai National Park in the middle of the upper Alaska Peninsula. If you have ever seen video of salmon leaping a waterfall and flying right into the mouth of a waiting brown bear, the site was probably Brooks Falls. When I worked there in 1972, the only access was via a riverside bear trail. Now there are park buildings nearby and an extensive boardwalk that allows hundreds of people per day to watch bears with minimal danger to humans and not much disturbance to the bruins. Nearby Margot Creek is also good.

Shelikof Strait and the East Flank of the Alaska Peninsula

While not so well known, and without the sheer density of bears, my own clients have preferred the more secluded experience of Katmai's eastern seacoast, along Shelikof Strait. Little of this terrain is accessible by plane except during the lowest tides (for beach landings) or during calm high tides (for oceanic landings). The best access is by skiff from one of the small ships that double as floating lodges—the finest way to see these coastal bears as well as seabirds and marine mammals.

Mount Douglas

Mount Douglas is the first in a chain of titanic glacier-sculpted mountains that jut out of the sea and rim the western shore of Shelikof Strait. This strait—about the width of the English Channel—runs between the Alaska Peninsula and the Kodiak Archipelago.

On Mount Douglas's eastern slope is Cape Douglas, a small peninsula that provides spectacular views of the peak. Other interesting features, just south of the cape, are two lakes that fill with icebergs calved off headwater glaciers. At least one of the rivers draining these lakes hosts a mid-September salmon run. The bears here are not accustomed to viewers and warrant extra caution.

Hallo Bay

South of Mount Douglas is Hallo Bay. The lodge at North Hallo, during certain times of the summer, provides easy access to nearby sites with good viewing. For the rest of the viewing season, clients are ferried to South Hallo, a true ursine paradise that offers sedge meadows where bears graze like cattle, as well as tidal flats where the bruins dig razor clams.

South Hallo is a great place to see rutting behavior during June. Mid-July is often a slack period with little food and few bears. In early August, when the salmon runs begin, viewing picks up again and continues into September. During those two months, however, other parts of the coast typically have larger salmon runs and thus more bears.

Kukak

Kukak Bay lies just beyond South Hallo. This is a good place to find scattered bears in early June, before they congregate on more exposed areas of the coast. During August and early September, up to a dozen bears fish near the river mouth of North Kukak River. On the extreme westward side of the river delta are two pinnacles of rock on which eagles nest. Elsewhere along shore is a scattering of small meadows where bears occasionally

Wolves and bears are competitors for some of the same food. This wolf has learned to harrass bears with fish, waiting until they drop their salmon to whirl around and face their tormenter. Then it darts in and steals the fish.

graze. Although bears might be seen foraging anywhere along the shore, attempting to view them on the west side of the bay is hazardous due to the huge extent of tidal flats where a boat or plane could easily be stranded by a swiftly falling tide. Near the mouth of Kukak Bay is Devil's Cove, the site of a lodge that caters to both anglers and viewers.

Kaflia

In early October of 2003, Timothy Treadwell and his fiancée were killed by a bear at their camp near Kaflia Lake's effluence into Kaflia Creek. Fortunately, none of the hundreds of other visitors to this premier viewing site have encountered serious aggression. The creek is reached by hiking inland from Kaflia Bay, following a short stream into Kaflia Lagoon, and then walking several hundred yards along the lagoon's northern shore—sometimes on land (struggling along a bear trail through dense alder thickets) and sometimes wading. Hip boots or chest waders are essential. It's not uncommon to encounter bears at very close range. While hiking, make plenty of noise to avoid surprising them.

Kuliak, Missiak, and Kiniak Bays

Continuing south from Mount Douglas, the next three bays—Kuliak, Missiak, and Kiniak—offer spotty viewing. Bears are found here only during salmon runs, which seldom last more than a week, and you will rarely see more than one bear at a time.

Geographic Harbor

The most popular viewing site on the Katmai Coast is Geographic Harbor, which lies at the back of a long and spectacular fiord that begins with Amalik Bay. Geographic Harbor offers experiences much like those at McNeil River in that viewers can sit on a grassy knoll and watch numerous bears catch salmon, play, or nurse cubs—sometimes at distances of 10 to 50 feet.

Chignik-Black Lakes, Ivanof Valley, and Unimak Island

There are mediocre viewing sites farther south on the eastern slope of the Alaska Peninsula, for instance at Ivanof Bay. Nevertheless, this is one

Volcanic Ash

Just west of the "Valley of Ten Thousand Smokes," there is a portion of Katmai Park that was virtually barren of plants when I first visited it in 1972. It had been buried in volcanic ash by the 1912 eruption of Mount Novarupta. The explosion was so powerful that it not only blanketed Kodiak Island, 30 miles to the west, but spread ash as far south as Seattle. Patches of this sandy ash are still visible, some of them so white that people mistake them for snow.

of the few potential viewing sites in Alaska that are served by regular—rather than charter—airplane service. The best viewing is on Ivanof River. Hike approximately 1 mile from the landing strip to the river, then another mile upstream. Keep in mind that these bears rarely see any non-Natives except trophy hunters, so they tend to be wary and upset by surprise close encounters. During the peak salmon run, starting in early to mid-July through August, expect to see at least a dozen different bears, but only one or two at a time.

Viewing is also spotty in the river system between Chignik and Black Lakes. This is one of the few areas where (silver/coho) salmon remain abundant throughout much or all of the winter. So long as this rich food source persists, some adult male brown bears remain active rather than hibernating. This provides a unique opportunity to see and photograph bears in winter. The best time is early September, during a year when bear hunting is not allowed in that area (many areas are hunted only in alternate years, or during spring of one year, then fall of the next year).

The permission of the Bristol Bay Native Corporation should be obtained. For Ivanof, check with the Kalmakof family. For the Chignik-Black Lakes area, consult a Chignik Lake phonebook.

Even more remote is Unimak Island, the first of the Aleutian Islands and a dormant volcano. This island is visited by few people indeed, largely because weather is often wet and windy; also, transportation costs can be prohibitive. Most people in these areas either live there or come to hunt bears. Hunted bears are not only harder to watch but more aggressive during surprise encounters. Nevertheless, if you want an ultimate wilderness experience, Unimak is one of the places to get it.

Western Flank of the Alaska Peninsula

Brown bears also abound on the west flank of the Alaska Peninsula. Viewing opportunities, however, are few and far between. Your best bet in this area is Becharof Lake.

Salmon reach that lake by swimming upstream from Bristol Bay through Egegik River. If you come during the height of the salmon run, you have a good chance of seeing numerous brown bears, although you may have to hunt to find where the bears and salmon are concentrated on any given day.

Kodiak Island

The Kodiak Island Archipelago lies due west of the Katmai Coast, across Shelikof Strait. Although Afognak Island and the northern part of Kodiak Island afford scattered opportunities for bear watching, most viewing occurs in the southern portion of Kodiak. The most popular area is Dog Salmon Creek, where salmon become vulnerable to bears as they wait to pass through a fish counter on their way upstream to Frazer Lake. After a short flight from the town of Kodiak or a remote lodge, you walk roughly 1 mile along a dirt road to the viewing area. There is a public-use cabin (space for six people) at Dog Salmon Creek that can be reserved for a short period if you apply in the spring (awarded by lottery).

Nearby Karluk Lake hosts one of the densest concentrations of brown bears on the continent. They have access to salmon in the Karluk River—which joins the lake to the sea—or near the head of the lake on Thumb or O'Malley Creeks. There is a lodge on Camp Island near the mouth of Thumb Creek. Land on both sides of Thumb Creek is owned by the local native corporation; so you must have their permit to access the site. The fish counter on O'Malley Creek was once a prime viewing site, but visitation is no longer permitted.

Brownies can also be viewed in several other areas of Kodiak National Wildlife Refuge, including Uyak Bay and the trash dump at Larsen Bay.

Kenai Peninsula and Prince William Sound

The western coast of the Kenai Peninsula bills itself as the "bear viewing hub of the world." It mainly serves as a departure point for boats or airplanes traveling to brown bear viewing sites on the Alaska Peninsula, or less often to black bear viewing areas along the south shore of Kachemak Bay, across from Homer.

There are better viewing opportunities on Kenai Peninsula's central portions, either at Juneau Falls or along the upper Kenai River or the Russian River. Juneau Falls is reached by a short hike up the Resurrection

Trail from the villages of Cooper Landing or Hope. You can often see bears by hiking along the northern bank of the Russian River. The lower section has a wide boardwalk that keeps you from walking in mud and makes it easy for bears and people to see each other at comfortable distances. Half a mile upstream from the mouth, you can ascend a high staircase to a parking lot and large campground or continue hiking upstream on a dirt path toward a small falls or all the way to Russian Lake. This is where you are most likely to surprise a bear at close range. A safer route is the mile-long shortcut from the road. The Russian River is actually a creek that flows from Russian Lake into the mighty Kenai River.

The Kenai River drains out of Kenai Lake, flows several miles westward to Skilak Lake, then drains out of Skilak and continues to the sea—a waterway world famous for its enormous runs of sockeye, king, pink, and silver salmon. Hiking along the Kenai River is discouraged because dense shoreline vegetation makes it hard to see bears before you stumble upon them. Viewing here is best done from a boat. Boats normally enter the river near the Russian River Ferry, then drift several miles downstream to the head of Skilak Lake.

Mountains around Cooper Landing are inhabited by Dall sheep and mountain goats—both of which may be seen even from the highway with binoculars or a spotting scope. Hunting is forbidden there, so you can sometimes climb to within photographic range of both species. This can also be a good area to see moose, especially in the wetlands between the river and highway.

Most bear viewing on the Kenai Peninsula occurs along its southeastern shore, accessed through the town of Seward. Black bears are occasionally seen close to Seward on the shores of Resurrection Bay, particularly in Thumb Cove. The best viewing, however, occurs in Aialik Bay, especially during May or June when bears feed in shoreside meadows. Aialik is part of Kenai Fiords National Park.

If you visit Seward, don't restrict yourself to bear viewing. Resurrection Bay is a great place to see orcas (killer whales), baleen whales, sea lions, seals, sea otters, and a wide range of birds. Along shore, you may also see Dall sheep or mountain goats. A few miles out of town, you can hike a mile to come within touching distance of Exit Glacier. Seward is also home to the Alaska SeaLife Center, which offers magnificent aquarium displays and live sea mammals and birds, as well as wonderful educational exhibits, videos, and lectures.

Halfway between Seward and Anchorage is the road to Portage Glacier. Unlike Exit Glacier (which is entirely on land), Portage Glacier ends in a lake, into which it calves icebergs. You can sometimes see scores of bergs floating there in all their myriad shapes and shades of blue or white.

The eastern shore of the Kenai Peninsula is accessed through the town of Whittier, which opens out into Prince William Sound. Many of the sound's numerous islands are inhabited by black bears and a few by brown bears. Although bears are occasionally visible on the beach, they are hunted during spring or fall and are wary of people, making viewing difficult. It is, however, a great place to see marine life and scenery, especially from a sea kayak or small boat.

Wrangell-St. Elias and Kluane National Parks

Between Prince William Sound and the Canadian border lies Wrangell-St. Elias National Park and Preserve. Continuing west into Canada are Kluane National Park and Wildlife Sanctuary. Although bears on the Alaskan side of the border have access to a small number of salmon each year, most of their diet consists of plants or scavenged meat. High mountains around the border deprive this park of much of the coastal rainfall. Conditions are even more arid on the Kluane side, where sagebrush abounds. This is one of the least productive grizzly habitats known. The bears are small, with low reproductive rates and reputedly short tempers. They are not brownies but grizzlies. Any attempt to view them should be done from inside a vehicle or at a distance of at least 400 yards.

Southeast Alaska

Although both black and brown bears are found along the coast of the "Alaska Panhandle," each of the hundreds of offshore islands normally has only blacks or browns, but not both. Brown bear populations occur only on Admiralty, Baranof, and Chichigof Islands. Most of the other islands normally host only black bears, although a few brown bears visit islands near the mainland.

Yakutat and Glacier Bay National Park

Due south of Kluane is the start of the Alaska Panhandle. Near its northern tip is Cape Yakutat. Nine miles outside the town of Yakutat, a road crosses the Situk River, providing a good opportunity to watch bears fishing. You can reach Yakutat by air from Gustavus or Juneau or by ferry (Alaska Marine Highway). From there, you can drive to Nine Mile Bridge. If you do not bring your own vehicle on the ferry, you can hire a taxi or join a bear viewing tour.

Roughly 60 miles south along the coast is Glacier Bay National Park, a maze of spectacular fiords and tidewater glaciers. Wave action and melting undercut the face of these glaciers, often "calving" huge icebergs into the sea. Beware: This calving action can create "tidal waves" large enough to swamp small boats or kayaks.

Although this park has no sites where you can count on seeing bears, both blackies and brownies are frequently seen on beaches. The park can be explored by sea kayak or on foot.

This park is one of the few places wherein you have even a remote chance of spotting a rare "glacier bear"—a black bear whose fur is tinged grey-blue. Almost as exciting is catching a glimpse of a wolverine, more common but very shy. You might also see wolves, Sitka deer, and moose, as well as sea otter, Stellar sea lion, harbor seal, northern fur seal, ringed seal, Dall's porpoise, orcas, baleen whales, and countless seabirds.

Admiralty Island National Monument

A half-hour flight from Juneau takes you to Admiralty Island National Monument and the Stan Price State Wildlife Sanctuary. Your plane will land in Windfall Harbor and taxi close to the beach, leaving you to wade ashore through a foot or two of water (hip boots or waders are a good idea; don't try it barefoot as the bottom is covered with sharp barnacles). A ¼-mile hike takes you to a gravel spit overlooking the mouth of Pack Creek where you can sit and watch brown bears grazing in the meadow or fishing for salmon

Stan Price

During the 1940s, Stan Price homesteaded the area encompassing Pack Creek. He learned to coexist peacefully with local wildlife, including brown bears, despite the attraction of these animals to his garden and groceries. He raised at least one orphaned cub and occasionally allowed it to visit inside his cabin even after the bruin had attained considerable size—much to the dismay of his two successive wives. Stan recognized and named over one hundred bears, some of whom featured prominently in the innumerable photos and movie footage he later used to educate people on how to live with brownies. Stan rarely if ever carried a gun, believing that he could deter any overly bold bear with his walking stick. In general, simply touching or tapping a bear with his stick was sufficient to keep the animal at least a few yards away. Only rarely was it necessary to deter a bear by beating it. The only time this failed and Stan was injured, the offending bear was a newcomer with whom Stan had not yet had a chance to develop mutual trust and respect.

(especially in July and August). Or you can hike another three-quarters of a mile inland to a viewing tower that accommodates up to eight people at a time, with a three-hour limit per person.

The Stan Price Sanctuary is operated jointly by the United States Forest Service and the Alaska Department of Fish and Game. Upon arrival, you will be greeted by a ranger who will acquaint you with the area and its rules, then answer questions. Rangers do not serve as guides or protect you from bears. Although you are allowed to carry a firearm or bear spray, in seventy years no one has ever been injured there by a bear.

About half the visitors fly in with a commercial guide who not only provides their transportation but also their viewing permit, hip boots, and perhaps pepper spray (guides will sometimes carry a firearm). Visitors who fly in without a guide must obtain their own permit. Only during the shoulder season, from June 1 to July 4, and August 26 to September 10, when visitors and bears are scarce, can permits be obtained on-site.

For visits during the peak season (July 5 to August 25), permits must be purchased and reservations made months earlier, preferably before March. Price varies with season and your age. Overnight camping is not allowed within the sanctuary but is allowed on either of the nearby islands, assuming that you have a boat to travel across the intervening water. This sanctuary encompasses only a small portion of Admiralty Island, which is inhabited by over 1,000 brown bears. Your best bet for an alternate viewing site is one of the coastal meadows on the eastern side of the island. Bears outside the sanctuary are hunted and viewing them can be difficult and perhaps risky.

Kupreanof and Kuiu Islands

Just south of Admiralty Island, across Frederick Sound, is Kupreanof Island. Near its northwestern tip is the village of Kake. Several streams within a few miles of town host runs of pink and dog salmon. These attract wary but viewable black bears. Surprisingly, the best viewing is often at Gunnuk Creek, which runs right through town, when dog salmon spawn below the local hatchery. That run coincides with the annual Dog Salmon Festival, a celebration not to be missed.

For a less urban experience on Kupreanof, Cathedral Falls is reached by driving several miles out of Kake on a rough gravel road, then hiking for a mile or so. The walk ends with a steep descent into Cathedral Gorge. Fish cannot ascend Cathedral Falls so they concentrate in a pool at the base of the falls where they are easy prey for black bears. Viewers can sit onshore and watch the bears chase live fish and scavenge dead ones.

Unless you arrive on the Alaska Ferry with your own vehicle, you will most likely have to depend on a local guide for transportation to a viewing site. Most guides are chartered by the tribe or city. Check with them for a guide or before attempting independent viewing. When I lived in Kake, black bears were also commonly seen at the town garbage dump—infinitely less aesthetic than a salmon stream but nevertheless a good place to observe ursid social behavior.

Kuiu Island lies a few miles east of Kupreanof, across Keku Strait. This strait is one of the few places in North America where giant squid have

Boat Safety

Chatham, like most of the other straits in the southeast, funnels through huge volumes of water in often unpredictable surface currents. Added to these are currents created by tidal rise and fall. Especially during periods when rapid tidal change is combined with strong winds, these waters can be extremely dangerous for boats.

been found (dead and decaying). Black bears occasionally swim the channel. Up until the mid-1990s, Kuiu received little hunting pressure and abounded in large blackies. Since then, it has seen both hunting and logging pressure. Although blackies are still reasonably abundant, they are not readily viewed.

Baranof Island and Lake Eva

Baranof lies due west of Kuiu across Chatham Strait. This island, like Admiralty to the northeast and Chichigof to the north, has a large population of brown bears. Although these bruins can be encountered in any of the countless salmon streams ringing the island, they're most readily observed at Lake Eva on the island's northeast corner.

Koskiusko Island

The next islands south of Kupreanof are Koskiusko and Prince of Wales. These islands are laced with logging roads and skidder trails. Where creeks have not been ruined by logging, they still host substantial salmon runs. There are no prime viewing areas here. However, if you carefully hike upstream from the shore, there is a good chance of spotting one or more blackies. They are also occasionally seen along the shoreline itself. Clams are highly abundant, but they and other shellfish play little role in ursine diets, perhaps because of the hazard of red tide during summers. Although these bears are generally no more aggressive than any other coastal blackies, some boars grow to enormous size, perhaps by resorting to cannibalism when fish are scarce. That the largest males may hunt

Author Stephen Stringham and photographer Kent Fredriksson both work as bear viewing guides. One of their company's two boats, MV Waters, *is shown here off Alaska's Katmai coast.*

and eat smaller bears is no indication that they would hunt a person. But be extra cautious around any large bear. And keep a sharp eye out for wolves—which are extremely shy but surprisingly abundant.

Anan Creek

Proceeding southeast across Kupreanof and Wrangell Islands, and past the towns of Petersburg and Wrangell, Anan Creek is another of the few places where you might potentially see both brown and black bears. Although bears are visible along most of the length of the creek, they concentrate at the falls where salmon are easiest to catch. Anan Creek hosts modest runs of chum and coho salmon, as well as one of the largest pink salmon runs in southeast Alaska (peaking from late June through late August). Bears can be viewed from *several yards away* while you stand on an elevated wooden platform—the Anan Creek Wildlife Observatory—hidden from the sight of bears, minimizing your impact and lessening the risk of conflict.

Visitors who fly into the region will probably find it most convenient to travel by commercial jet to Ketchikan, then by floatplane to Anan. Visitors who arrive by ferry might find it more economical to disembark at Wrangell or Petersburg before boarding a floatplane or a charter boat for the final 30 miles or so to Anan Creek. After landing, it is approximately a ½-mile hike to the observatory. Although most of the hike is across a gravel trail or boardwalk, it begins by crossing a beach of large cobbles and rocks.

Anan Creek empties through Anan Lagoon into Anan Bay, near the mouth of the fiord known as Bradfield Canal. It is recommended that boats and floatplanes not enter the lagoon even at high tide. Not only is there danger of the craft being stranded as the tide drops but vehicle activity may drive away bears and other wildlife. Boat travel to the lagoon maximizes your chance of viewing marine mammals, although it takes longer and may reduce the time you can spend at Anan.

At Anan, a ranger is on duty to assist you. Only sixty-four visitors are allowed per day. Permits are obtained from the Forest Service, Tongass National Forest, and Ketchikan/Misty Fiords Ranger District. To maximize your chances of obtaining a permit, apply early, preferably by March. If you fly in on a commercial tour (but not on a charter), your guide will provide your permit.

Margaret Creek, Traitor's Cove, and Neets Bay

The next major island south along the coast is Revillagigedo. At its northwest corner are Neets Bay and Traitor's Cove. These are fine places to see black bears at close range during August and September, and their nearness to the city of Ketchikan minimizes travel costs. They are just a twenty-minute flight across Revillagigedo Island or a several-day kayak paddle if you have the time and skill. For faster water travel, take a jet boat.

Whether you're a fisherman, hiker, or bear viewer, when walking along an Alaskan salmon stream, there is always the risk that you might stumble upon a dozing or distracted bruin.

Arriving at the cove, you enter the small inlet where Margaret Creek empties into the sea. From there you have a 1-mile walk (or van ride if you've flown in with a tour company) up a logging road beside Margaret Creek, and then a ¼-mile hike to the bear viewing observatory platform. The site accommodates only a few people at a time and is accessible by permit only. Permits are obtained from the Forest Service, Tongass National Forest, and Ketchikan/Misty Fiords Ranger District. If you fly in on a commercial charter, your guide will already have a permit.

Misty Fiords National Monument

Separating Revillagigedo Island from the mainland is a fiord known as Behm Canal. This fiord forms, for more than 50 miles, the western boundary of

Misty Fiords National Monument, a region of spectacular gorges and titanic glaciers. Midway up this fiord, on its mainland side, is Rudyerd Bay. At the head of the bay is Nooya Estuary, draining Nooya Creek. It's conveniently reached by plane, kayak, or boat from Ketchikan and offers spectacular scenery as well as heavy use by brown bears in late summer during the major salmon run. It has not been improved for bear viewing and is not normally visited by tour groups. Camping is discouraged.

The monument's western boundary is the Portland Canal, a 70-mile-long fiord that also forms the southern border between Alaska and Canada. This canal ends at the junction of two rivers, one flowing out of Canada, the other—the Salmon River—flowing out of Alaska. At this junction is the Alaskan town of Hyder, a community of less than 200 residents. Just a few miles away is the larger town of Stewart, British Columbia. Both towns can be reached by Canada's Stewart-Cassier Highway or by a forty-minute flight from Ketchikan.

Just a few miles up the Salmon River from Hyder are the mouths of Marx Creek and Fish Creek. Wildlife observatories at these creeks are just a short hike off the road and offer opportunities to see both brown and black bears. As bears fish for spawning pink or chum salmon from July through September, they can be viewed from several yards away by visitors standing on an elevated observatory—allowing superb close-up photos at minimal risk. (Further protection is provided by rangers armed with shotguns and pepper spray. Although viewers are rarely injured, one man camping near the town dump was killed by a brown bear several years ago.)

Visitors who fly in can reach the observatories by tour bus or taxi. At the height of the season, these observatories are visited by a few hundred viewers each day. They lie within the Tongass National Forest and are managed by the USDA Forest Service, Tongass National Forest, and Ketchikan/Misty Fiords Ranger District. Bears are seen mainly on the Salmon River and its tributary creeks, although some venture out onto the tidelands. You might also expect to see beaver, mink, or wolves, as well as a variety of birds including bald eagle, harlequin ducks, Canada geese, common mergansers, herons, and a diversity of songbirds.

Coastal British Columbia

Proceeding southwards along the Pacific coast into Canada, one finds few good viewing areas, in large part because so much of the coast has been logged of old-growth forest. The sole surviving pristine watershed, the Khutzeymateen Valley, lies just south of Portland Canal and is accessed by boat or plane from Prince Rupert. All viewing is done from a boat; viewers are normally not allowed to go ashore. Bears are seldom seen from distances of less than a few hundred yards.

Approximately 100 miles father south is Princess Royal Island, which hosts the largest concentration of white-colored (Kermode) black bears, also called "spirit bears." Out of roughly 130 blackies on the island, almost 10 percent are white. The Alaska Marine Ferry passes beside this island in the Princess Royal Channel on its way between Seattle and Prince Rupert. To reach the island, leave the ferry at the village of Bella Coola. A tour boat will take you the rest of the way. This boat, or a small lodge on the island, can serve as your base of operations. You might get lucky and spot a spirit bear on your first day. But some people wait two or more days before seeing any bear of any color. Only the luckiest viewers have close encounters with a spirit bear. Boat tours from Bella Coola may also provide glimpses of black-colored blackies in other parts of the region, as well as a wide variety of marine mammals and seabirds.

The next prime viewing site is down near Vancouver Island. Knight Inlet is a long glacial fiord that penetrates deep into the mainland. This is the closest place to the United States where you can watch brown bears, as well as the largest concentration of brown/grizzly bears in southern British Columbia. To see these bears, you can join a tour boat from Vancouver or book into a lodge within the inlet.

Bears are seen nearly every day. Your viewing chances are best during the spring when bears graze, court, and mate in shoreline sedge meadows or during the salmon run (late July through late August) when they concentrate on a stream. During the run, you might be able to view from the safety of a platform or tree stand. Otherwise, nearly all your observation will be done from a boat, cruising up and down the inlet looking for bruins. Close-up photos are possible but not an everyday event. Bring the most powerful telephoto lens you can afford and good binoculars. After the salmon run tapers off, bears continue scavenging fish carcasses along shore for another month.

There are also plenty of opportunities to see black bears among the region's countless small islands, especially during low tide when the bruins forage for intertidal invertebrates. This is one of the best areas on the coast for seeing orcas and other marine mammals as well as seabirds.

Garibaldi Provincial Park

Farther south on the coast, near Canada's border with the United States, is the city of Vancouver. Sixty miles north of Vancouver by road, or somewhat longer by boat (up Howe Sound and the Squamish River), is Garibaldi Provincial Park. At its northwest corner is the resort town of Whistler, famous for its Blackcomb Ski Area. Although the park is home to grizzly and black bears, as well as mountain goats and deer, the bruins are normally only glimpsed from afar. You may have better luck seeing the bears that join the thousands of bald eagles to harvest salmon in the Squamish estuary. Your best bet for seeing black bears is on the ski slopes during summer. This is reputedly one of the best black-bear viewing sites on the continent.

Interior of Southern Canada and the Contiguous U.S.

Sierra Mountians and Yosemite National Park

California's crown jewel national park is renowned not only for its spectacular glaciated valleys but for its black bears. There are no prime viewing sites. Spotting bears is a matter of luck—good luck if you are hiking and want to watch bruins, bad luck if they invade your campsite. There is no population of black bears more famous for its banditry. Be extremely careful in how you store food! Blackies can also be glimpsed at Kings Canyon and Sequoia National Parks and even in the town of Mammoth, as well as around Lake Tahoe.

Rocky Mountains

Grizzly and black bears are occasionally viewable in the mountain parks of Canada (Kluane, Jasper, Banff, Glacier, Waterton-Glacier, Kootenay, and

For most bear viewers, the chance to sit inconspicuously and watch bears interact in natural situations is much more rewarding than insisting on asserting your presence.

Yoho Parks) as well as in the lower forty-eight states in and around Glacier and Yellowstone National Parks. There are currently more than 1,200 grizzlies south of Canada, most of them in Glacier and Yellowstone, along with a hundred or more south of Glacier and in tiny remnant populations near the Montana-Washington and Canada-Washington borders. Black bears can be seen in several western states, including California's Sierra parks and nearby communities such as Lake Tahoe and Mammoth. For the recreational bear viewer, however, these habitats offer little in the way of guarantees.

Minnesota

Northern Minnesota offers excellent viewing opportunities for black bears. One hundred and twenty miles north of Duluth, near Orr, Minnesota, the Vince Shute Wildlife Sanctuary receives roughly 500 visitors

Every potential bear viewer should articulate what he or she wants to take back from the experience. Finding a guide who can safely put you in position to take close, "nostril-shot" pictures is a rare thing.

per day. Visitors park away from the viewing area and are bussed to an elevated viewing station that provides superb visibility. It is considered one of the best places anywhere for observing black bear social behavior. There is a small daily user fee.

Not far east of Orr, at Ely, Minnesota, the new North American Bear Center promises to become the world's finest facility dedicated to educating the public about bears. Orphaned or injured bears will be cared for there and rehabilitated for return to the wild. These bears will be visible from an elevated platform or bear-level observation windows. Bears resting beyond direct view or hibernating in dens will be visible via remote video. The main building will provide static and video exhibits, a lecture area, a children's center, reference library, classroom, gift shop, and minitheater.

There will also be outdoor exhibits to teach campers and residents about coexisting with bears. Exhibits will include a model campsite, demonstrations of bear deterrents, and displays of bear-proof garbage cans, dumpsters, food containers, and bird feeders. Markers along nature trails will point out bear sign, food plants, and other components of bear habitat.

A more natural way of getting to know black bears is possible about 15 miles into the wilds from Ely at the Wildlife Research Institute. Instead of catering to crowds, the institute focuses on bringing small groups of people into more intimate contact with bears. The institute's director, pioneering black bear biologist Dr. Lynn Rogers, provides unique opportunities for visitors to come within touching distance of bears and to walk with them in the woods during advanced classes on bear ecology and behavior. While somewhat expensive, this is an experience no bear lover should miss.

Riding Mountain National Park

This park, located in central Manitoba, lies on the Manitoba escarpment, an area of rolling hills that rise out of a sea of agricultural lands. It contains a small population of black bears that can be glimpsed now and then. Beware that they have a reputation for being more aggressive than is typical for the species—on a par with black bears in northern British Columbia, Yukon Territory, and Interior Alaska. The park is also home to a substantial wolf pack, as well as lynx, fox, moose, elk, deer, and (captive) bison.

Eastern Provinces and States

Farther east, black bears abound in Ontario's Algonquin Park, New York's Adirondack State Park, Virginia's Blue Ridge Mountains, and the Great Smoky Mountains National Park of Tennessee and North Carolina. In these areas, don't expect to find groups of bears consistently at specific sites, except perhaps trying to raid food coolers in a campground. Count yourself lucky if you catch even a glimpse of a bear running through the trees. Your best chances to see black bears in these areas are in groves of nut trees during fall. Algonquin is also known for its populations of moose, deer, lynx, and wolves.

MAKING THE MOST OF YOUR TRIP

CHAPTER 7

CHOOSING A GUIDE

If you're considering an excursion specifically devoted to bear viewing, the first question to ask yourself is if you need to hire a professional guide. Having worked as a viewing guide for some years, I'm obviously biased. I would argue that a professional guide can make your trip easier, more comfortable, and almost always more successful. There are situations, for instance, when your personal safety may depend upon a knowledge of bears and bear behavior unavailable to most typical outdoor enthusiasts. If a bear runs at you, is it inviting you to play or is it threatening you? Is it even attacking you? How do you respond to defensive threats such as woofing, pant-huffing, jaw-snapping, or ground-swatting (the ursine equivalents of cussing)? Any amount of aggression is scary, and there's never a guarantee it won't escalate. Having a 700-pound bear charge forward a couple of body lengths and smash both paws against the ground while woofing explosively is an experience most of us would

Even the most skilled bear is lucky to catch a salmon more than once in every ten tries. Having missed this time, the bear stands poised to strike again.

rather not have. Guided viewing puts a minimum amount of responsi-bility on your shoulders and doesn't require you to know much about bears or safety (although being versed in both can add greatly to your enjoyment).

A good guide will also know about other wildlife in the area and be able to offer advice for the best places to hike, fish, kayak, or simply go on a picnic. A guide can help you refine your list of needed equipment and supplies and in some cases can provide rain gear, hip boots, etc. Given that so much of the best bear viewing occurs in national parks and monuments or in state sanctuaries, a pro guide will also know how to acquire the necessary permits. In fact, some guides are allocated a cer-tain number of permits for specific sites, which they can then pass along to their customers. This may be the only way of obtaining a permit if you apply after February.

A professional guide will know where bears can be found during each season and under various conditions of weather and tidal level. He or she should have enough experience at a site to know which individual animals will allow you to get close enough for good viewing. Some bears feel crowded at distances that other bears tolerate. Bears with ready access to escape terrain may be more tolerant than those whose only escape routes would bring them too close to other people or more dominant bears—factors a professional guide should watch for. The guide should also be able to judge when a normally good site isn't quite right. Windy days tend to make some bears nervous and thus less tolerant during sur-prise close encounters. On the other hand, some sites or bears may be best approached only when the wind is blowing from you toward them, warning the bears that people are coming.

While you focus on watching and photographing bears, a good guide will keep track of everything else going on around your group. He or she should remain aware of changing conditions such as wind direc-tion and strength, tidal level, or shifts in the numbers and locations of bears. The guide's equipment should include cans of pepper spray and waterproof flares, as well as a VHF radio, emergency locator transmitter, or satellite phone.

Once you have decided to hire a viewing guide and have perhaps chosen a region and time of year for your excursion, the next step is to find a guide that suits your particular circumstances. To begin, you might consult books and magazine articles relevant to the area. A bear-savvy author or photographer may make a superb source of information. Or you might try the ever-dependable Internet. In most cases, a Web search won't lead you to an individual guide but to a guiding service. Unfortunately, if the service typically employs a number of guides, they may not know beforehand which guides will be working for them that season, much less which will be on duty that particular day. Expect to be told that all their guides are good. It's best to be politely skeptical and ask specific questions about guide qualifications and certification. Before booking, don't be afraid to ask questions. For instance,

- How many bears am I likely to see during a typical day? Will these primarily be boars, sows with cubs, or adolescents?

- What sort of bear behavior am I likely to see during this time of year and in this location? Will they be digging for roots or grazing on sedge grass? Will they be digging for clams or catching salmon? Will they be courting, sparring, or nursing?

- How close can I expect to come? What percentage of the time will be spent within 50 yards of bears? 100 yards? 250 yards?

- Will I have a clear line of sight to the bears, or are the animals likely to be obscured by brush or trees or, worse, other viewers?

- Will the bears be aware of me? Will my presence disturb them?

- As I photograph, will the conditions be good? Will the sun typically be at my back? Will it be convenient to set up a tripod or monopod for steady photos?

- If it rains or snows, what kind of clothing and shelter will be provided? If viewing from a vehicle or observatory, does it have a roof and/or walls?

- Will I be in a situation that requires rubber boots or waders? Will the guide provide them? If I'm hiking, how far will I go and under what conditions?

To prevent the bears from feeling threatened, note how these viewers are clustered together and removed from the bears by natural platforms.

- Are there any situations where the group will be without a guide?

- How will the guide stay abreast of weather changes? How will he or she communicate with base or transportation (boat or plane) in case of an emergency?

- What are the guide's qualifications? Is he or she versed in bear safety, natural history, first aid, and education? Is the guide an employee or a contractor? What liability insurance and/or bonding covers the guide? If the guide is certified, then by whom and according to what standards? How many years of experience with bears? How much of that experience was gained hunting bears or researching them?

This last group of questions is particularly important. In the absence of governmental certification standards, guides differ greatly in their expertise on bears. Anyone who can sign up clients and get close to bears can call himself or herself a guide.

Some bear guides working in the summer also guide hunters during spring and fall. This can work well in that hunting guides tend to be savvy about wildlife and are usually well equipped with planes, lodges, and other visitor accommodations. Many other guides are simply pilots or captains who operate a vehicle for carrying people close to viewing sites. Less common are guides who began viewing bears out of fascination for the animals, then turned their hobby into a profession. Rarest of all are those professional wildlife biologists, usually bear researchers or managers, who came to guiding after retirement or who guide as a summer break from teaching.

If you are coming to your viewing experience with a strongly held set of beliefs regarding hunting or the environment, you should also ask after your guide's personal philosophy. If a guide disagrees with a worldview that you hold dear (if he is a hunter, for instance, when you dislike hunting), it can spoil even the best viewing opportunity.

CHAPTER 8

TRAVEL TIPS

Most Alaskan viewing sites are accessible only by hiking after traveling on a plane or boat. There are a few locations where your craft will bring you to within viewing distance of bears, but most bring you no closer than a ¼ mile. Rarely will you have to walk more than a mile over rough or steep terrain. Before booking a tour, make sure that you know how you'll be traveling to and from the viewing site and how strenuous the trip will be. Be sure and tell your guide about any physical limitations you might have so that he or she can make special arrangements to meet your needs.

You can drive to within several miles of most viewing sites in the Lower Forty-eight (including those in Yellowstone, Glacier, Yosemite, and Great Smoky Mountains National Parks). In Alaska, however, the only good viewing sites approachable by road are those in Denali National Park, Yakutat, Hyder, Kake, and Cooper Landing. Virtually all the rest have

Author Stephen Stringham inadvertently approached Kent Fredriksson as Kent was photographing this young bear; even the most seasoned experts can sometimes make mistakes (in this case, potentially "trapping" the bear between two viewers).

to be approached by aircraft or boat. You can drive to Kake and Yakutat, although only by putting your car on the Alaska Marine Ferry. Once in Kake, you can drive a mile to Gunnuk Creek or a few miles to the trail to Cathedral Falls. From Yakutat, you can drive 9 miles to the Situk River Bridge.

Flights to a remote viewing site are usually in a small "bush" plane, such as a DeHavilland Beaver or Otter or a Cessna 206. There's no better way to see Alaska's incredibly vast panorama of glaciers, ice-carved peaks, and rumbling volcanoes than from the air. You'll almost certainly want to photograph during the flight. (A tip: Since taking photos from a plane usually requires the pilot to circle with his side of the plane tilted down—so he can see the wildlife he's circling—the best spot is usually a seat directly behind the pilot, preferably at a window not obstructed by a wing strut.)

Most small aircraft windows are not glass but Plexiglas, which makes them vulnerable to scratches. In case your window is dirty, you might want to carry a small bottle of Windex and a paper towel. Especially if you are on the side of the plane towards the sun, beware of glare and reflections. I was recently dismayed to find that my video of a flight was marred by dim reflections of my bright yellow float coat. The darker the clothing you wear, the less likely you are to see yourself reflected in your pictures.

When professionals take aerial photos, they sometimes use a semi-rectangular frame to fit the window or door opening. One style of frame has four bungee cords, each with one end hooked to a corner of the frame, and all running to a ring at the center. When the camera or camcorder lens rests in the ring, the bungees smooth out vibrations from the plane and protect against jerkiness caused by air turbulence. Personally, I've never gotten that elaborate. Any vibration and jerkiness that can't be eliminated by my camcorder's stabilizer system can usually be compensated for on my computer with video editing software.

Whatever bush flying you do in Alaska should be done with a professional pilot. The extremes of glacially cold mountains and hot lowlands, coupled with fog banks and storms that materialize out of nowhere, always make flying in Alaska a risk. During 2003 only two Alaska bear viewers (Tim Treadwell and Amie Huguenard) were killed by bears whereas six

Small bush planes, capable of landing on ice, water, or even gravel bars, are to Alaskan travel what taxi cabs are to New York. It's difficult to do anything in the Alaskan backcountry without utilizing their services.

viewers in the same area were killed in a plane crash. Be aware as well that many popular viewing areas are inaccessible for one to three days at a time, and you may have to wait out bad weather before making or returning from your trip. To prepare for such delays, its best to incorporate a few spare days into your trip plan.

I seldom ride in a bush plane without wearing a float coat and carrying a lap pack with an emergency locator transmitter, VHF radio or cell phone, signal mirror, smoke bombs, and survival kit. In Alaska and Canada, most bush planes carry emergency supplies (at least a sleeping bag and pad for the pilot's personal use) as well as an emergency locator transmitter (ELT) designed to activate automatically in the event of a crash. The ELT I carry in my pack flashes and makes an audible burst of static every time it broadcasts a distress signal.

As you're flying, keep in mind that it is ethically (and, in most cases, legally) suspect to fly over wildlife at altitudes that will disturb the animals. I try not to pass lower than 500 feet. Even if your plane is close for only a few seconds, the emotional stress on the animal can last for hours, and the effects of several planes per day can measurably impact the health of a population. I was once nearly overrun by a grizzly fleeing from a diving Cessna, and a local man was mauled by a grizzly that had just fled from a low-flying plane.

Of course, there are a number of places a plane can't land, and the expense of flying can be prohibitive. Tour boats allow unparalleled opportunities to watch marine mammals and other sea life, and they are significantly safer than aircraft. If they are enclosed, they also offer refuge in case of sudden bad weather. The best boats are essentially floating lodges.

Travel between an ocean-going boat and shore is done in a skiff. In a boat, as in an airplane, every effort should be made to avoid disturbing wildlife. The potential for disturbance depends on how the boat is handled, the loudness of its engine, and its speed. An outboard motor up to fifty horsepower doesn't bother most bears if the boat approaches or passes them slowly. By contrast, airboats and hovercraft are especially bad. Both employ huge aircraft engines, which produce tremendous roars that can panic bears or other animals and send them racing away.

As you spend time viewing along the coast, make sure a falling tide doesn't strand your boat or airplane; and make sure a rising tide doesn't wash away your craft or trap you against a cliff or on an island. Although a skiff or pontoon boat is great for getting you close to bears, they are unstable and not ideal for photography. There is seldom room on board for a tripod, but a monopod can be invaluable.

When choosing a boat, and if your main objective is viewing, try to join a group wherein everyone else shares that same objective, rather than one where some of the people want to fish. Nothing rocks a skiff worse than an angler struggling to land a large salmon.

Hiking

Aside from Wolverine, Tuxedni, and a few other sites where you can watch bears from a vehicle, most viewing is done while you are afoot. Once your boat or floatplane has landed, it may deposit you directly onshore, or you may have to wade some distance. On a seashore with sand or mud-flats, and especially if the tide is falling, you may have to wade for as much as a ¼ mile.

Nearly all trails to bear viewing sites were created by the bears them-selves. Don't be surprised if one of the "construction crew" expects to have right-of-way. So long as a brown or black bear has plenty of warning that you are in the vicinity, it will likely either detour around you or allow you to retreat off the trail to give it free passage.

As you're hiking, when crossing streams or navigating potentially dangerous mud or quicksand, a walking stick can be invaluable. I like a tough telescoping monopod that I can also use to steady my camera.

Overnighting

One of the most frequent complaints I hear from clients is, "I wish that I could have stayed longer." Most half-day trips last no more than five hours, often counting the time spent traveling. That can leave you with no more than one to three hours to watch bears. At some sites, during the seasonal peak, that's plenty of time to photograph bears at reasonably close range. At other places or during the off-season (at Wolverine Creek, for instance, during early June or late August), a half-day trip provides no more than a fair chance of *glimpsing* a bear, and a poor chance of seeing several bears for even half an hour. One of the worst scenarios for a bear viewing guide is to watch a group of clients who've just spent a big chunk of their savings for "the adventure of a lifetime" fail to view even a single bear. Even a single full-day trip may not meet your needs.

For a multiday trip, you've got to select somewhere to overnight. One option is to overnight near town, then return to a viewing site day after day. You don't need to get more than a few miles out of most Alaska towns to be in relatively wild and scenic country where there's a chance

Bear milk is thicker than whipping cream (up to 25 percent milk fat), and cubs seldom let any go to waste. After nursing, they lick any leftovers off of Mom's breasts and even off one another's lips.

of seeing a moose or caribou or a wide range of waterfowl and songbirds. This is also where you'll find a broad selection of stunning lodges, many of them large log structures.

Some lodges close to a remote viewing site offer rustic luxury, but most are a lot more rustic than luxurious. You might have to settle for having an unadorned cabin, simply a place to be warm and dry with hot meals. This may not sound like much, but compared to camping in bear country in inclement weather, it could be heaven.

There are a few lodges (at Wolverine Creek, Crescent Lake, Silver Salmon, Glacier Meadows, Clearwater Creek, North Hallo Bay, Devil's Cove, Camp Island, Kake, and Hyder) that are located so well that you are virtually guaranteed good viewing during the seasonal peak. However, most remote lodges have a significant shoulder season, wherein you may be lucky to even glimpse a bear.

Some lodges offer you no other viewing options during the off-season (for example, Wolverine Creek) while a few (North Hallo Bay) cope with the shoulder seasons by flying you back and forth to seasonally better sites. Other lodges (there is one at Devil's Cove) ferry you to alternative sites in a skiff or pontoon boat.

To my way of thinking, the best kind of "lodge" is one that moves when and where the bears do. I prefer an ocean-going boat. Clients typically will arrive by floatplane, then spend a few days using the boat as their "base camp." The finer boats have comfortable cabins wherein you and your gear can stay warm and dry while charging camera batteries, cleaning equipment, etc. Everyone eats together in the galley, providing opportunity for lively conversations and fascinating bear stories from your guide. For evenings and stormy periods, most boats will offer a small library of natural history books and novels, as well as videos.

I don't recommend camping near a viewing site. No matter how experienced you are at camping in the wilderness, your conventional precautions likely aren't up to the challenge. For example, how do you avoid camping near a bear trail when the land around you is literally laced with bear trails? It's usually not a matter of whether a bear will visit your camp but more of *how many* bears will visit. Everything you do, every object you have, and every odor wafting from you or your camp could arouse the interest of a bear.

CHAPTER 9

ESSENTIAL EQUIPMENT AND SUPPLIES

Clothing

Alaska is a land of extremes, even from May through September when nearly all viewing takes place. Bringing the appropriate clothing is essential to an enjoyable experience and can sometimes mean the difference between life and death. Hypothermia has killed many more people than have bears.

A breathable Windbreaker is important, as are rain pants and jacket to keep yourself dry even while walking through wet brush. Your rain jacket or poncho should have a hood to keep your neck dry. Wear a baseball-style hat to keep rain and the jacket/poncho hood out of your eyes. Neoprene gloves will keep your hands warm, wet or dry.

Both black and brown/grizzly bears come in an amazing range of colors. The blackish "basalt" brown bear, like the boar shown here, is one of the rarer color phases.

Choice of foot gear is more complex. If you won't be wading streams or tidal waters, you probably won't need rubber boots. In that case, wear shoes that are reasonably waterproof. High-tops are the best. If you can't do that, then slip on a plastic bag between your socks and shoes. Carry extra socks so that as your feet become soaked with water or sweat, you can switch to a dry pair.

If you're wading, wear either hip or chest waders. If your tour guide doesn't supply them, you'll have to bring your own or do without. For crossing streams or intertidal zones paved with slimy rocks, I put cleats on my wader boots. I like the Get-A-Grip brand. It has tiny metal spikes that provide good traction on most surfaces.

If you are lucky enough to do your bear viewing during one of Alaska's uncommon clear and warm days, you should also remember to bring sunblock and good sunglasses, preferably with polarized lenses.

One of the most essential items, of course, is an adequate supply of bug dope. Alaska is famous not only for its mosquitoes but also its black-flies, white-socks, no-see-ums, and other little nasties. Different bugs tend to be repelled better by one kind of repellent than another, and while there's no one brand that works against all bugs equally well, I like to carry Ben's or OFF! When browsing bug repellants, look for the active ingredient Deet. I would recommend avoiding Skin-So-Soft, as anything with a per-fumed odor may be even more attractive to bears than it is to you.

Bear-Resistant Food Containers

If you are going to be watching bears only for a few hours, it's wise to avoid carrying any sort of food or drink except water. For longer trips, when carrying food is necessary, it should be stored in plastic bags that are sealed to minimize the leakage of odors. The bags themselves should be stored in bear-resistant containers. The plastic barrels I've seen have a capacity of one to two gallons.

Steel barrels are heavier than plastic, but come in larger sizes. Those in the two- to ten-gallon range can be backpacked. Barrels with bear-proof locking mechanisms are also available in sizes up to fifty-five gallons.

A good bear photographer needs to come prepared for any exigency. For shooting in high winds, a collapsible monopod is a good idea. It can also be used as an emergency walking stick.

Photography

When it comes to cameras and binoculars (remember to take them!) how much lens power you'll need depends on how close you are likely to be to the bears. Before you pay to join a guided tour, shop around and ask each potential guide or tour company about viewing distances. Typically, a single bear isn't likely to fill your frame if you have less than a 300 mm length lens for a 35 mm camera or 8x binoculars. (To estimate the power of a 35 mm lens, divide its length by 35. Put differently, a 10X lens on a digital camera or binoculars is roughly equivalent to a 350 mm lens on a 35 mm camera).

Your guide should also have ideas about the best film to use. At most viewing areas in Alaska, the sky will usually be overcast. If you are using a lens longer than 300 mm, you'll need ASA 200 or 400 film; with a longer lens and dimmer light, you may need to push it up to 1600. Of course, the faster the film the grainier the final image. (Be aware as well that at some viewing areas you may be forbidden to use a flash.) If you prefer a digital camera, make sure your system recharges itself within a small fraction of a second, and that you have several high-speed secure chips for recording images.

Since most bear viewing occurs near water, it's also advisable to equip your camera with a polarizing filter to counteract glare.

Unless you carry a range of films and multiple cameras, you might appreciate the greater flexibility allowed by the newest digital cameras. Some get good pictures even in bright light with heavy contrast or in dim light with minimal contrast. Cameras with at least five megapixels and fovea sensors give good results; these are available for under $200. Even a ten megapixel camera with an ultrasharp lens is now priced under $500.

Digital cameras use up a lot of battery power, however, so *carry lots of extra batteries* and storage memory. Sure, that sounds obvious, but you'd be amazed at the number of times my clients end up running out of battery power or memory even during the first hour or two of viewing. Come prepared to take a few hundred shots per day.

During lulls in viewing, review your shots so that you can discard any duds—leaving more memory for better pictures. Some people carry a small hard drive into which they can download pictures as they go. There are also small battery-powered printers on the market that can produce postcard-sized prints shortly after you take a photo. Other people download to the Web as soon as they get back to civilization.

Most electronic devices are ultrasensitive to moisture; cameras are no exception. Three or four continuous days of rain can compromise the equipment of even the most conscientious photographer. In most situations, a raincoat for your camera can quickly be constructed from a plastic bag and duct tape or glue-on strips or tabs of Velcro. When not shooting, store your camera inside one or two layers of sealable plastic bags, preferably with a sack of silica gel to remove all moisture from the air inside the bags. Keep the camera protected even indoors lest warm moist air enter the camera, then later condense when you go outside into colder temperatures.

When I'm in the field, I like to carry all camera gear and other optics in a "dry box." I avoid the brands specifically designed for cameras as being too heavy for backpacking. Instead, I prefer a plastic box with an O-ring sealing lid of the kind designed for anglers and boaters. These usually have a capacity of one to three gallons. For hiking, I carry two three-gallon dry boxes strapped one above the other on a pack frame. While viewing, I sit on the lower dry box and use the pack frame as a backrest. The other dry box is in front of me, where I can extract or insert the camera or camcorder at a moment's notice.

Although some newer cameras and most newer digital video recorders contain built-in stabilizing mechanisms, a strong Alaskan wind or moving vehicle is still going to introduce blur into your images. When you're inside a vehicle or an observatory, there may not be enough room to extend the legs of a tripod, and if you need to yield immediate right-of-way to a bear, a tripod may prove too cumbersome. For these and other reasons, I usually prefer a monopod.

In dense brush like this willow thicket, it can be hard to avoid surprising bears at close range—one of the greatest dangers faced by any hiker. This photo was taken near Katmai's Kaflia Creek not far from where Timothy Treadwell and Amie Huguenard would later be killed.

CHAPTER 10

MINIMIZING RISK AND IMPACT

Even as an experienced guide, it should be said that I don't fully trust any bear, and moderately trust only those I've known for months. Hiking through dense brush along a salmon stream, my heart still races and my palms still sweat at the possibility of bumping into an irate bruin. I'm at least as cautious with even the most "friendly" bears as I am while driving on glare ice. The smart bear viewer takes every precaution to minimize risk, then learns how to cope with what remains. Bear viewing at close range shouldn't be seen so much as a test of your guts and skill as a test of the willingness of bears to tolerate you. Your challenge as a viewer is always to avoid causing problems, not to seek them out.

Whatever your reason for watching bears—whether to take photos, learn about the animals, or cultivate a sense of kinship—you don't want to be injured, and you shouldn't harm or disturb the bears. To do this most efficiently, there are a few basic rules to follow, some of which I've already mentioned in passing but all of which deserve to be reiterated.

Depending upon a bear's familiarity with people, the time of year, and the circumstances of the viewing, each animal maintains its own "crowding zone." As a bear viewer, you can only come so close to a bear before it starts to feel crowded. You and your guide should take all precautions to avoid violating this zone. You can do this by studying the bear for signs of agitation and by reading the body signals it sends.

Groups of three or more people are generally safer than individuals, but too large a group also has a greater probability of disturbing and displacing bears. In many cases, a group of five to eight people is ideal. Members of a single viewing group should stay within a few arm's lengths of one another. If there is more than one group in an area, you should also come together to form a single group. Bears are apt to perceive a greater threat from two or more scattered groups than from a single cohesive group.

In places where people regularly visit, consistent use of the same sites makes humans more predictable for bears and thus may help minimize disturbance. People should also avoid going so close to prime bear feeding areas (fishing sites, for instance) that they interfere with feeding. Use of an established trail may also make human movements more predictable to bears. When going to and from viewing sites, it is usually best to be visible and wary. Brushy surroundings that are used as resting and secure areas by bears should be avoided, or at least approached with caution, making noise to alert any nearby bruins.

If a bear is approaching, you should take care to avoid blocking its path. If it is clear that the bear is interested in you and not just walking past, you should assert yourself to define and defend your own crowding zone. Assertive actions should begin innocuously, such as by holding one's ground (not moving away from the bear), raising one's arms and waiting, speaking to the bear, and perhaps standing on a higher object. If the approach continues, your actions should escalate appropriately. This is especially important with younger bears who shouldn't have the opportunity to learn that they can push people around.

Protecting her cubs, a mother bear (right) roars at a boar who ventured too close. Both bears lower their heads to signal willingness to settle the matter without fighting—even as their gaping mouths and exposed canine teeth demonstrate an ability to defend themselves.

Alaskan bears tend to ignore bells, whistles, and most other artificial sounds. Although some bears ignore the sound of an air horn, others pay keen attention and may even steer clear of it. I personally prefer breaking branches or sticks, clapping my hands three to five times in rapid succession, then perhaps calling out something like "Helllooooo" in a singsong manner.

Although many experts argue that talking makes enough noise to alert most bears at a safe distance, I don't recommend it. Talking or listening to other people distracts you from watching for bears.

Reading and Mimicking Bear Etiquette

Bears have a certain body language that they use with each other and, to a certain extent, with bear viewers. If you know what to look for, you can often tell when you are behaving badly as far as the bear is concerned.

Closely bonded bears—a mother and her cubs; a group of siblings; or a few friends—usually approach one another directly and calmly, often with ears and eyes focused on each other. Direct approach by any *other* bear, however, especially by one with its ears and eyes *locked* on target, is often taken as offensive, provoking either withdrawal or threat. Offensive aggression is confirmed if the approaching bear lowers its head and pins back its ears as it gets close—signaling that it's willing to fight, but also giving its target the option of submitting or withdrawing.

By contrast, a benign, curious approach by a mere acquaintance or stranger tends to be indirect, as the approaching bear seems to just drift or zigzag towards the target, usually grazing along the way. A peaceful bear's head is usually at feeding height and its ears open to the sides, neither flattened against its skull nor focused on the other bear. Aside from brief head-high glimpses at the stranger, a peaceful bear does most of its watching with its head low, using peripheral vision.

Peaceful bears may eventually graze past one another with only a brief pause, then drift apart. After repeated passes like this, perhaps over a period of hours or days, the two bears may gain enough mutual trust to approach with their heads higher and come close enough, nose to nose, to smell and touch each other, then eventually to play.

I approximate some of these same methods (for example, avoiding eye contact and approaching obliquely) when I approach bears that can see me coming from a fair distance. If I am determined to get close to a wary bear that seems not to have noticed me, I usually try alerting it long before I could crowd it—say no closer than 200 yards in open, coastal terrain or 300 yards in inland habitat (add another 100 yards when your visibility is impaired, for instance by vegetation or topography). If a coastal bear doesn't seem wary and is likely to have had many peaceful close encounters with viewers, I may approach to within 150 yards before tailoring any closer approach to its behavior. I never stop monitoring for signs that the bear is aware of me and that it might be becoming agitated. If a bear is approaching me in a curious or bold fashion (versus being blatantly aggressive), violating my own crowding zone, there are a number of techniques I try to utilize. Each can be performed by a lone person but they work best when done by a group. I prefer beginning with the least provocative defenses and escalating only as necessary—progressing through techniques in roughly the following order.

If a bear is approaching me from the side, it may stop if I turn to face it. I may also speak to it in the same kind of quiet tones one uses to soothe a frightened child or dog. If I'm sitting down as a bear approaches, I may rise to my knees or to my feet. This signals that I'm feeling crowded. Most bears comply by coming no closer and perhaps by moving farther away. If I'm in a group of people, and if we are somewhat scattered, I ask that we all close ranks, forming one unified body to face the bear.

Occasionally a bear can be distracted by tossing something past it (although *not at it*). I've seen this done with a ball-shaped float lost from a marine fishing net. When this landed in front of the bear and rolled past, the bear followed to investigate, much as a dog or cat might. This broke the bear's concentration on the viewers. However, do not throw food, your pack, or anything else that might reward the bear's boldness!

If none of the above techniques halt a bear's approach, viewers may use firm tones to tell the bear to stop. Or they might deter approach by imitating huffing and jaw-popping. Especially those bears already familiar with people may recognize either sound as a way of mimicking ursine signals for, "Please don't come closer."

If you surprise and aggravate a bear at close range, you might be able to calm it a bit by quickly letting it know that you aren't another bear, perhaps by doing something that no bear would do, such as waving your arms. This can be especially effective if you have a plastic garbage bag in hand, filling it with air and waving it overhead. Abruptly shouting something like "Stop!" is a tactic some guides have used several times, but I use it cautiously. It can potentially escalate the aggression.

If a strong "Please!" or "Stop!" doesn't work, I may take matters to the next level of ursine threat by imitating a bear's hop charge, stepping or jumping forward one pace and stamping a foot hard while woofing explosively and clapping my hands as loudly as possible. There is a risk, however, that even this low level of threat can backfire and provoke a bear. I use it only when necessary.

If none of the above measures deters a bear, I might walk or run a few steps toward it, stamping my feet while shouting loudly and waving my arms. This is best done by a tight group.

As a last resort (short of using a deterrent device or weapon), you might use a walking stick to distract and disconcert a bear, waving it in front of the bear or imitating a bear's swat threat by rapping the stick against the ground or perhaps breaking branches. I've seen bears retreat from a wildly flopping salmon so why not from a wildly pounding stick? It should be said, however, that a stick is far more effective as a psychological deterrent than as a weapon. Unless a bear was attacking, I would never strike it. But if attacked, I would strike as fast and hard as possible. Better yet, I'd use pepper spray.

Recognizing Aggression

One of the main factors determining the level of a bear's aggressiveness is competition for food. Rivalry can at times be so intense that bears have little tolerance for intrusion even by other bears, much less for people. Competition is worst in habitats with a short growing season—for instance in the high Rockies or Interior Alaska—where winter can last more than nine months. The fewer months bears have for stocking up fat for winter the harder they have to push during summer, and the farther you need to stay from them to avoid provoking or disturbing them.

Coastal bears have it easier. The growing season is one to two months longer than in interior habitats at the same latitude. Furthermore, the well-watered coastal lands offer rich supplies of berries and other succulent plant foods, and the ocean provides an abundance of salmon and other marine meats. Close to the ocean, food is usually so abundant

During August and early September, coho salmon swim into Geographic Harbor before fighting their way upstream through a gauntlet of brown bears. Note the group of viewers at the far right, keeping a respectful distance.

that bears don't need to fight for it. Big bears may usurp the best fishing sites and choicest tidbits, but even the lowest-ranking bears seldom starve. It's not at all uncommon to see a dozen or more coastal brown or black bears digging clams, fishing, or grazing within 50 to 100 yards of one another. High tolerance for fellow bears may carry over to high tolerance for people.

No matter the bear species or the situation, it's a lot easier to avoid being mauled if you learn how to read a bear's signals and respond properly. Understanding ursid motivation and perception can be critical to determining how to behave in order to protect yourself.

Many people have referred to the "bluff charges" that bears make. This is a term I dislike. Bluffing implies that an animal doesn't have the means or the will to follow through. Instead, I prefer the term "threat charge." The bear is trying to win by intimidation—by making you so afraid that you won't dare attack it, or perhaps so afraid that you won't be able to defend yourself if *it* attacks.

In a hopping threat charge, the bear hops towards you, rearing up slightly and slamming its paws into the ground. Most hop charges continue for only a few hops, but sometimes they carry the bear along much farther, with the bear's body slightly sideways towards you. They almost never end in attack.

Less often, a bear approaches you at a run. Whether it will stop or veer away before contacting you is difficult or impossible to predict.

Prior to a charge, bears will often reveal their anxiety by pant-huffing—a series of huffs interspersed with inhalations *huh-aah-huh-aah*. The faster and louder the huffs, the more intense the stress. A sequence of pant-huffs often begins with a *woof*—a single explosive release of air, analogous to the snort of a deer. Peak aggression is signaled by bellowing or roaring. If a bear's fear is vastly outweighed by its aggression, its head will be held high and it may roar much like an African lion. If fear is nearly as strong as aggression, the bear's head will be held low and its roars will pulse like this: *arh-arh-arh*.

Bears also snap their jaws, a sound accentuated by popping the lips as the mouth opens after each snap. The sound may occur either rapidly or slowly, depending on the degree of stress. At low stress, you may hear only a slow clunking of the jaws, without any lip pop. They may also threaten by biting objects or ripping chucks of wood out of a handy tree trunk, or by clawing or swatting the ground or some object such as a tree, perhaps breaking off branches or saplings.

If you are close enough to study a threatening bear's face, you may look to see how it's holding its mouth and jaws. In a low-level threat, the front of the lip is puckered slightly forwards (still hiding the upper canines) and the jaws are closed or slightly open. In an intense threat, the upper lip (and perhaps the lower lip) is extended as far as possible, and the jaws are gaping, fully revealing the upper and lower canines.

Not unlike a dog, bears sometimes show their level of threat by the way they hold their ears and head. The head held high, ears cocked forward, signals confidence. Only in the moments before attack are the ears of a confident animal flattened against the skull. By contrast, a dog or bear that is both highly aggressive and highly fearful may have its ears pinned back and its head held low. A lack of obvious threat signals does *not* mean that a bear is at ease with you—merely that it is confident of being able to handle you should the need arise. To distinguish high confidence from tolerance, you need to look for more subtle clues.

If a bear shows "white eye" (a rim of white or bloodshot sclera on the outside edge of its iris), it could be an indication of agitation and intolerance. If a bear is approaching or circling you with its ears flattened against its skull and its head low, it's most likely giving you a warning sign. Agitation can also be presented in the form of a "cowboy walk"—strutting past or toward you with forelegs stiffened and perhaps stomping the ground with its "hands," perhaps while urinating or defecating. Doing this with the elbows turned out and hands turned in somewhat resembles the gait of a bow-legged, pigeon-toed cowboy. This posture is usually associated with head-low threat. There is also the "sumo strut," wherein the bear walks past or toward its opponent with hind legs stiffened and swinging wide, usually while urinating. The bear may stop every few steps and wiggle its hindquarters back and forth, grinding its urine scent into the soil. This may be done with the head high or low and the ears usually forward, not pinned against the skull. Whereas a cowboy walk may preface attack, a sumo strut is merely an expression of dominance.

The greater the number of vocal or gestural threats that are shown by a bear, and the greater their intensity and duration, the more likely that the bear perceives its target as a danger to itself or its companions, or as a rival for dominance or resources—not as prey.

Polar bears are somewhat different in their body language signals and vocalizations. For example, among polar bears, threat charges are made mainly by sows with cubs or by young bears of either sex, not by adult males. When a boar polar bear charges, it is likely attacking.

Appeasement Signals

Not all bears that approach you present themselves as a threat. A bear that is shy but curious might investigate you by drifting towards you as it forages, watching you only with peripheral vision. It might even stop now and then to sniff the ground, as though investigating scent marks left by another bear. Once close to you, the bear might lift its head to see you better, but continue watching out of the corner of its eye. I know of no case wherein a bear has acted this way just prior to an attack.

If a bear approaches while keeping you in sight, with its ears cocked in your direction, you should look for additional clues to identify its mood and intentions. Is it simply confident and curious (as in hundreds of cases wherein a bear approached me that way), or is it highly dominant and trying to intimidate you?

Apart from those very rare cases when bears are being specifically predatory (in which case they are unlikely to exhibit any visible threats, much less appeasement), grizzly/brown bears that are being protective tend to be the most dangerous of all bears, especially if they are surprised at a close distance. A protective bear can usually be distinguished from a competitive or predatory bear by the situation (e.g., a sow with small cubs) and by its signals, especially pant-huffing, jaw-snapping, lip-popping, threat-walking towards the intruder, or hop-charging, and perhaps long-charging towards the intruder. A protective bear may retreat then charge, retreat, then charge.

I try to appease protective bears by showing them that I'm no threat. While I don't retreat during a charge, I may do so very cautiously between charges. I have successfully retreated when a bear threat-walked towards me, but only long enough to make clear my willingness to appease the bear; if it had kept following me, I would have stopped and stood my ground.

Bear experts generally advise you not to run from any bear unless you are sure of reaching a refuge. Once most people start running, they panic and can't stop. Running usually increases your fear and tends to rob you of self-control.

Landy, a well-known female, stands in the Russian River of the Kenai Peninsula, watching for migrating coho salmon.

Surviving an Attack

Only as a last resort—with all other options explored and with a protective or competitive bear about to make contact—would I drop to the ground and "play dead."

If you are forced into that position, you should be certain to protect your face, throat, and neck. Lie facedown with your hands laced behind your neck, elbows out to the sides. Keep your legs widespread, making it harder for a bear to roll you over and thus expose your stomach. If you get rolled, try to keep on rolling until you end up facedown again. A poorer way of playing dead is to roll into a ball with your face between your knees and hands behind neck. If you are wearing a backpack that doesn't contain food, keep it on to provide partial protection to your neck.

Before resorting to playing dead, you will hopefully have used the can of pepper spray you remembered to bring with you. In my opinion, this is the most practical and effective deterrent available. Be careful to use only those sprays recommended against bears, since cans designed to repel people or dogs may not have sufficient volume or potency. Even brands designed for bears vary in their burn power, in how long they last, and in how far they shoot. Those under the greatest pressure shoot farthest, but are exhausted soonest, and vice versa.

Before you are likely to encounter a bear, test your can to make sure it works, and to observe how the pepper spray behaves in the air—how far it shoots, how long it hangs, and how readily it is blown away from your target area. Remember that you have only ten seconds or so of spray in the can so make your test shots as brief as possible.

Spray comes out in a conelike shotgun pattern, narrow at first but spreading rapidly. Ideally, your first press of the trigger should be as brief as possible so that you can see where the spray goes. With luck you might have time to adjust your aim before pressing the trigger again. Once your aim is correct and you are trying to stop a bear, don't keep the trigger down for more than one second at a time.

To further minimize wastage of spray, I would delay my pepper shot until the bear was reasonably close. If it were walking towards me and I felt threatened, I would not shoot until it was within 20 feet, or perhaps even 10 feet. If it was charging, however, I'd start blasting when it was about 50 feet away. Even though the spray itself won't go farther than 30 feet, a bear can run 15 yards per second. By the time a bear had cut the distance from 50 to 30 feet, a cloud of spray should be hanging in the air to greet it. Only after a charging bear was within 20 feet might I hold the trigger down until the bear stopped or swerved aside. If the bear continued its charge and was definitely going to maul me, I would tuck the pepper spray to my chest, drop to the ground, and play dead—then hope to blast the bear right in the eyes and mouth. This has worked for some victims.

I personally carry two cans of spray. One can is holstered on a chest harness and one is on my belt. The belt can may be quickest to reach,

What kind of pepper spray should I use?

There are two basic kinds of pepper spray: oily and oil-free. There are several brands of oily spray on the market, each containing capsicium oil squeezed from hot peppers, then diluted with vegetable oil. This mixture is known as oleo capsicium (OC). Beware that the percentage of OC is not a good guide to the burn power of a spray. Some sprays have a lower percentage of pepper oil than others, and some pepper oils are much hotter than others.

Once you spray with OC, residue may end up on the ground, vegetation, your camp, or your person. Unfortunately, this residue can be attractive to some bears. To get around that problem, Kate and Cody Dwire invented an oil-free spray. This apparently does not attract bears and it may provide more burn power than the same amount of OC spray. Testing is still under way to determine whether there are any conditions (e.g., rainy weather) when OC spray is preferable. The oil-free spray I tested was very effective.

Until the oil-free spray hits the market, your only option is an OC spray. The only brand I trust is Pepper Power (www.udap.com).

aim, and fire without removing it from its holster. In fact, many people can fire faster and more effectively with a can of spray than with a firearm.

Pepper spray isn't necessarily reliable at temperatures below forty degrees Fahrenheit. Before depending on spray under these conditions, test it to see how far it shoots and how long the spray hangs in the air.

CONCLUSION

A trio of siblings watches from a riverbank while their mother fishes. Most prime sows have two or three cubs at a time. Adolescent or aging sows are more likely to have only one or two cubs.

CHAPTER 11

CONCLUSION

Early August. Salmon were still scarce, but it was one of the lowest tides of the year. Several groups of tourists had flown in to Katmai from Kodiak Island and the Kenai Peninsula to watch these Hallo Bay brown bears spend the morning digging for razor clams.

Not wanting to disturb either bears or bear viewers, I approached to within 20 yards behind one of the groups, waiting quietly for half an hour until the people moved on, leaving me with a clear view of a blond sow who had just finished nursing her two small cubs. Gently, I moved forward to the vacated spot, sat down, and pulled out my camcorder.

I glanced up from my video camera just in time to see the sow roll off her back onto her feet and start walking directly at me, nervous youngsters in tow. Wondering what the blazes was going on, I switched on the camcorder, then sat quietly. To my surprise, the sow walked past just an arm's length away. Proceeding to the spot where

I'd been standing, she sniffed it for a few minutes, then started back. Only as she passed me a second time, then laid down in her original spot, did I recognize her. This was Kara, Lorca's oldest daughter. I had been following her life since she was less than six months old. I'd last seen her a year earlier when, as a newly matured adult, she had tried to take refuge behind me and my viewing clients to avoid the amorous advances of a boar named Snagletooth.

Being caught between two brown bears had been neither fun nor safe. Shooing her away, my clients and I had moved off to give the "loving" couple more room.

Fortunately, my rudeness back then hadn't left her with a grudge. Best of all, here she was with two new cubs, coming over to check me out. This was clearly a sign of recognition—which my late friend Tim Treadwell would have taken as a greeting. This is not how bears normally behave around people.

As if my encounter with Kara at low tide wasn't enough to make my day, high tide provided another memorable experience. By that time, I had linked up with a group of viewers led by Lynn Rogers—a very skilled biologist who's been studying bears since the late 1960s.

To escape the rising tide, we'd settled on the highest knoll in that region of Hallo Meadows, waiting to be picked up in our skiff and ferried back to the waiting tour boat. Meanwhile, we weren't the only ones who didn't want to get inundated by the tide. Kara's four-year-old sister Lala swam over, climbed the knoll, and laid down just a few body lengths away. Her sense of place was so exact that even at peak tide, the water rose to within just 2 inches from her body before the tide turned and began ebbing away. Meanwhile, cameras and camcorders had been working overtime, taking photos of Lala lounging in front of us like a Rubenesque nude.

These aren't the kinds of experience you can plan for. But they are certainly among the most memorable, when animals can share our lives without fearing aggression from us or giving us a reason to fear them. Indeed, it was not fear that Lala evoked, but a deep and thrilling peace

Snowball, a rare "ghost griz," or white-phase brown bear, at age two years, photographed in Katmai's Hallo Bay.

that made our spirits sparkle and bubble like champagne. Visions of majesty, moments of grace. It's what bear viewing is all about.

With enough luck, consideration, respect, and care, experiences of a similar sort might be available to you as well.

Sites and Opportunities to Watch Grizzly/Brown (G) or Black (b) bears

Location	Bear Species	View From	Overall Quality	Risk	Transport Mode	Lodging	Access Town or City
Cook Inlet							
Alaska Wildlife Conservation	G, b	F, a	**	*	a	L	Anchorage & Portage
Wolverine Creek	G, b	B	***	*	A	L	Soldotna or Anchorage
Tuxedni Bay	G, b	F, B	**	*	A	L, C	Soldotna or Homer
Silver Salmon	G, b	F, U	***	*	A	L, C	Soldotna or Homer
Glacier Meadow on Chinitna Bay	G, b	U	***	*	A	L	Soldotna or Homer
Chinitna Bay - West & South Shores	G, b	F	*	*	A	L	Soldotna or Homer
Chinik Creek	G	F, U	***	*	A, B	C	Soldotna or Homer
McNeil River State Game Sanctuary	G	F, U	****	*	A, B	C	Soldotna or Homer
Alaska Peninsula							
Funnel & Moraine Creeks	G	F	***	***	A	C	Soldotna or Homer
Douglas River Mouth	G	F	***	***	A	C	Soldotna or Homer
Wood Tikchik Park	G, b	F, B	**	***	A	L, C	Dillingham
Katmai National Park							
Brooks River	G	F, P	****	*	A, B	L, C	Homer or King Salmon
Shelikof Strait	G	F, U, B	****	*	A, B	L, C	Homer or Kodiak
Swikshak Lagoon	G	F, B	****	*	A, B	C	Soldotna, Homer, or Kodiak
North Hallo Bay	G	F, B	****	*	A, B	L, C	Soldotna, Homer, or Kodiak
South Hallo Bay	G	F, B	****	*	A, B	L, C	Soldotna, Homer, or Kodiak
Kukak Bay	G	F, B	****	*	A, B	L, C	Soldotna, Homer, or Kodiak
Kaflia Bay & Creek	G	F	****	*	A, B	L, C	Soldotna, Homer, or Kodiak
Kuliak Bay	G	F, B	****	*	A, B	L, C	Soldotna, Homer, or Kodiak
Missiak Bay	G	F, B	****	*	A, B	L, C	Soldotna, Homer, or Kodiak
Kiniak Bay	G	F, B	****	*	A, B	L, C	Soldotna, Homer, or Kodiak
Amalik Bay & Geographic Harbor	G	F, U, B	****	*	A, B	L, C	Soldotna, Homer, or Kodiak
Chignik-Black Lakes	G	F	**	***	A, B	C	King Salmon & Chignik Lake
Ivanof Valley	G	F	**	***	A	C	King Salmon & Ivanof
Unimak Island	G	F	**	***	A, B	C	False Pass or Cold Bay

		Quality	Viewing From	Risk While Viewing	Regional Transport	Lodging & Meals	Access From
Kodiak Island							
Karluk Lake & River	G	**	F, B	*	A	C	Larsen Bay & Kodiak
Thumb Creek near Karluk Lake	G	***	F	**	A	L, C	Larsen Bay & Kodiak
Frazer River/Dog Salmon Creek	G	**	F, B	**	A	C, c	Larsen Bay & Kodiak
Uyak Bay	G	**	F, B	**	A	C	Larsen Bay & Kodiak
Kenai Peninsula							
Kenai & Russian Rivers, June	G, b	***	F, B	***	A, a	L, C	Cooper Landing or Soldotna
Ressurection Bay & Aialik Bay	b	* to ***	F, B	*	A, a	L, C	Seward
Prince Wm. Sound (e.g., Olsen Creek)	G, b	* to ****	F, B	*	A, a	L, C	Whittier, Portage, or Anchorage
Southeast Alaska							
Glacier Bay	G, b	***	F, B	*	A, B	C	Gustavus, Juneau or Yakutat
Situk River near Yakutat	G, b	**	F, a	*	A, B	C	Gustavus, Juneau or Yakutat
Alaska Chilkat Bald Eagle Preserve	G, b	**	F, B	*	A, B	L, C	Haines
Chilkoot Lake State Recreation Site	G, b	**	F, B	*	A, B	L, C	Haines
Admiralty Island	G	****	F, B	*	A, B	C	Juneau or Angoon
Stan Price Wildlife Sanctuary	G	**	F, I	*	A, B	C	Juneau
Baranof Island (e.g., Lake Eva)	G	***	F	*	A, B	L, C	Sitka or Angoon
Gunnuk Creek (in Kake)	b	***	F	*	A, B	L, C	Juneau or Petersburg
Cathedral Falls (near Kake)	b	***	F	*	A, B	L, C	Juneau or Petersburg
Kuiu Island	b	***	F	*	A, B	L, C	Juneau or Petersburg
Hyder Estuary	G, b	***	F, B	**	A, B	L, C	Ketchikan, Hyder, or Stewart
Fish Creek (near Hyder)	G, b	***	F, I	**	A, B	L, C	Ketchikan, Hyder, or Stewart
Marx Creek (near Hyder)	G, b	**	F, I	**	A, B	L, C	Ketchikan, Hyder, or Stewart
Traitor's Cove (Margaret Creek)	b	**	F, I	*	A, B	CD	Ketchikan
Neets Bay & Creek (at wier)	b	**	F, I	*	A, B	CD	Ketchikan
Rudyerd Bay (Nooya Estuary)	G	****	F, B	**	A, B	CD	Ketchikan
Anan Creek	G, b	****	F, I	**	A, B	CD	Wrangell or Ketchikan

KEY

Viewing From a = auto, B = boat, I = improved observatory (e.g., platform), U = unimproved observatory, F = free ranging on foot

Regional Transport Transportation to the general region, a = auto, B = boat or ship, A = Aircraft

Quality: * = mediocre **** = superb (Based on access to bears, the variety of activities likely to be seen, and the likelihood of good weather.)

Risk While Viewing at photographic distance, * = low, **** = dangerous

Lodging & Meals C = camping OK, CD = camping dangerous. L = lodge or hotel or motel near viewing site

ABOUT THE AUTHOR

Dr. Stephen F. Stringham has studied bears since 1969, focusing on population ecology, communication, aggression, imperiled populations, and rearing orphaned cubs. He has also studied moose and other ungulates, as well as marine ecology. He is director of the Bear Communication and Coexistence Research Program and of the Bear Viewing Association. He is an adjunct professor at the University of Alaska, where he teaches wildlife courses, including bear safety. Dr. Stringham is also the author of *Beauty within the Beast: Kinship with Bears in the Alaska Wilderness.*

Bear with us!